Reader's Digest

the green home

Hundreds of practical ideas
for eco-friendly living

Reader's Digest

the green home

Published by The Reader's Digest Association Limited
London ✽ New York ✽ Sydney ✽ Montreal

contents

HOME-GROWN FOOD

Getting started

Here are hundreds of easy ways to protect your family's health, save you money and safeguard the environment by making your home greener.

What is green living?

We all want to lead happy, balanced lives. We want to feel fit and well, save money on household bills and have a positive effect on the environment. By adopting a green approach to living, you can achieve all of this.

Invariably the green approach will simplify your life while saving you money on shopping and household bills. For every tip you adopt, you are making a difference to the environment – whether it is saving energy and water, cutting down on air pollution or adding less to landfills.

For instance, did you know that the air in the average household can be up to three times more polluted than the air outside? A major contributor to this pollution is the arsenal of chemical cleaners used in most homes. But you don't need all those expensive products when versatile natural products will do the job just as well. Bicarbonate of soda, for example, can be used to clean the oven, polish the kitchen sink, unblock household drains, deodorise furnishings and carpet and remove stains from linen.

What can you do?

Start making changes slowly. Next time you buy toilet paper, buy a brand made from recycled, unbleached paper. Next time you need to replace a light bulb, try out a low-energy compact fluorescent lamp – as well as helping the environment, you'll also save money on your energy bills.

GREEN LOGOS

If you buy a product labelled with one of these logos, you can be assured that the product has been produced in such a way as to minimise its environmental impact, whether it's food that has been grown organically, wood that has come from a sustainable source or an appliance which has been designed to save energy.

Soil Association

Organic Farmers & Growers

Organic Food Federation

The Forest Stewardship Council – The Mark of Responsible Forestry

European Union Ecolabel

The Energy Saving Recommended logo for the most energy-efficient appliances

Refuse plastic bags when you shop. Use cloth bags instead – most supermarkets sell cloth or synthetic bags that can be used over and over again. In the UK, an estimated 17 billion plastic bags are given away by supermarkets each year. So next time your newsagent starts to pop your favourite magazine into a plastic bag, ask them not to.

There are also more expensive purchases you could consider avoiding or recycling. For example, many people in the UK discard their mobile phones every 18–24 months when they buy a later model. This results in millions of mobile phones going to landfill and releasing nickel and other metals into the soil and groundwater. But the phones can be recycled and the batteries can be melted down and made into other products.

So before you throw something out – whether it's a glass jar or an item of furniture that's seen better days – consider whether it can be reused or recycled, or given away.

At home, if you have no room for a sprawling vegetable garden, think about growing organic herbs and a few salad vegetables on your balcony or windowsill. You'll always have fresh herbs for cooking and the ingredients for a garden salad, they'll cost you next to nothing and you can be happy in the knowledge that they are safe to eat.

Why not start making some easy, stress-free changes now, and save yourself money and time as well as lead a healthier, safer life? This book has all the advice you need and also includes a useful directory of green suppliers and organisations for further information.

the
natural
home

Y ou'll create a healthier, more comfortable home if you select
natural materials and efficient appliances, and adopt energy
and water-saving habits. You'll also help the environment
and save dramatically on living costs. The room-by-room survey in
this chapter suggests strategies to make each part of your home
more energy-efficient and safer to live in.

Efficient living

Careful use of natural resources will save you money and create a healthier, more comfortable home as well as helping the environment.

Energy-efficient home

Using less energy around the home is much easier to achieve than you might think. Reducing heat loss to a minimum, making simple design changes, choosing and using your appliances wisely, and changing a few old habits can make all the difference to your energy bills, your comfort and to the environment.

Top ten energy savers

1 Make sure that your home is well insulated. A properly insulated home can be up to 10°C warmer in winter and as much as 7°C cooler in summer.

2 Whenever the weather permits, use a clothes line instead of a tumble dryer to dry your washing. You'll save money and help to reduce greenhouse gases by about 3 kilograms for every load of washing.

3 One of the simplest ways to save energy is to switch off appliances at the wall when you won't be using them for a few hours. Keeping appliances on stand-by can account for 10 per cent of a household electricity bill.

4 If your central heating has an adjustable thermostat, try turning the heating down a degree. You may not notice much difference in temperature, but you could make big savings: a reduction of 1°C can reduce bills by as much as 10 per cent.

The energy we use each day accounts for about half of the UK's carbon dioxide emissions

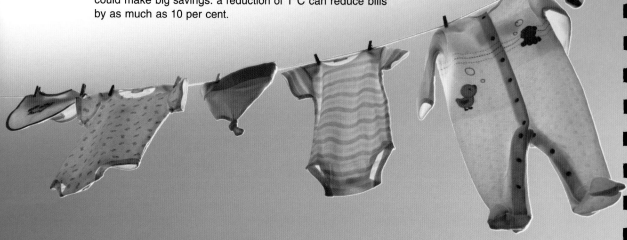

HOUSEHOLD ENERGY USE

More than half of the energy used in an average home goes on heating the house and the hot water. Any energy-saving measures implemented in these areas will have a big impact in reducing the overall energy consumption – and the fuel bills, too.

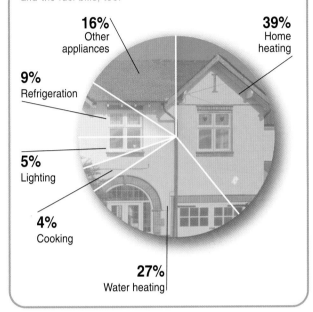

16% Other appliances

39% Home heating

9% Refrigeration

5% Lighting

4% Cooking

27% Water heating

ENERGY RATINGS

Today it's easier than ever to compare the energy efficiency of similar products thanks to a range of energy labels. By law, the EU energy rating label must be shown on all fridges, freezers, washing machines, washer-dryers, tumble dryers, dishwashers, electric ovens and light bulb packaging.

● WHAT IT MEANS The EU energy label rates products from A (the most energy efficient) to G (the least efficient). Reflecting advances in energy efficiency, the rating goes up to A++ for fridges and freezers.

● THE BENEFITS Most properties on the market now have to include Home Information Packs (HIPs). Buyers will receive detailed information on the energy efficiency of a home with a rating of A to G. Houses with a good rating will sell quicker. Properties with a poor rating may be eligible for grants to improve their energy efficiency. For more information, contact the Warm Front Hardship Fund (see page 122) or your local council.

5 Plug gaps around windows and doors, and any other external openings, using draught excluders. Draughtproofing can cut household heat loss by up to 25 per cent in winter.

6 Reduce heat loss by up to one-third in winter by covering windows with heavy, lined, close-fitting curtains and a closed pelmet.

7 Replace standard incandescent light bulbs with low-energy compact fluorescent lamps (CFLs). Although a little more expensive than conventional bulbs, energy-saving lightbulbs are much more efficient, lasting between 6 and 15 times longer than standard bulbs and using 80 per cent less electricity. Replacing a standard 100W light bulb with a 20W low-energy bulb can save around £12 per year in electricity costs.

8 Select appliances that are both energy-efficient and the right size for your needs – a 284-litre fridge will use 20 per cent more energy than a 210-litre fridge, even if they both have the same energy rating.

9 Make sure that your hot-water tank and pipes are properly insulated with lagging. In an average home, heating water accounts for more than one-quarter of the household energy bill; and as much as half of total water-heating costs can be due to heat loss.

10 Switch to a green energy supplier. They buy a percentage of electricity from renewable sources and switching could cut your carbon footprint by nearly 6%.

energy saving
recommended

The most efficient appliances carry the Energy Saving Recommended logo, so look out for this when deciding what to buy.

Insulation basics

The key to improving energy efficiency and cutting utility bills is to make sure your home is properly insulated. Good insulation will keep heat inside in winter and help to keep your home cool in summer. It could cut your heating bills by up to 50 per cent – and improve your home's efficiency rating for when you come to sell it.

Getting started

Before you start take a look around your home for the potential causes of heat loss and work out what you can do about these. Remember, there are grants available for installing cavity wall insulation or double-glazing for which you may be eligible. Check with your local council or call the Energy Saving Trust or Warm Front Hardship Fund (for contact details, see page 124).

● **Factor in long-term savings.** Overhauling your home insulation may seem expensive and time-consuming, but it can pay for itself in under five years in reduced heating bills.

● **If you have existing insulation that is inefficient,** consider adding another layer to improve its performance. Aim for at least 270mm thickness of loft insulation (the minimum required by Building Regulations in new builds).

● **Make sure you insulate all areas of your home** – walls, floors, loft and windows. A 5 per cent gap can reduce potential benefits by up to 50 per cent.

● **To maximise the effects of insulation,** shut off all air outlets, such as chimneys and vents, when not in use.

● **Ensure that all hot-water tanks and exposed pipes** are well insulated with specialist lagging. As much as half of the total water-heating costs in an average home are due to heat lost through poor insulation of pipes and tanks.

About **half of the heat** lost from an average home **disappears through the walls and the loft**

Insulation materials come in a variety of different forms, from loose fill to batts and rolls. Using these materials to insulate your home could make it as much as 10°C warmer in winter.

Selecting materials

There are two main types of insulation materials, which can be used either separately or together.

● **Reflective insulation is usually made from aluminium foil** laminated on to paper or plastic. It works by reflecting and resisting heat. It is highly effective at preventing summer heat gain via the roof.

● **Bulk insulation works by trapping pockets of air,** which in turn inhibit heat flow. It can be made from various materials including glass fibre, wool and cellulose fibre, and comes in several forms such as batts, loose fill and boards.

● **Some products combine the two types:** for example, you can buy foil-backed blankets or foil-backed batts.

● **There are many natural and efficient insulation materials available.** These include Thermafleece (made from wool), Warmcel (recycled newspaper) and Isonat (made from hemp and recycled cotton).

Adding insulation

Loose fill is used mainly for flat ceilings and confined spaces. Batts and rolls can be used for ceilings, pitched roofs, walls and floors. Look for biodegradable materials with no health risks.

● **Avoid loose-fill bulk insulation** if your roof space is draughty; alternatively, apply a sealant to its top surface to hold it in place.

● **Keep bulk insulation dry at all times.** If condensation is a problem, fit a 'vapour barrier' – usually reflective foil – on the warm side of the insulation material. Installing roof vents will also help.

● **Don't install insulation within about 90mm** of heating flues or on top of, or within 25mm of, recessed light fittings.

● **When working with glass fibre and mineral fibres,** wear protective clothing and a mask as the fibres can irritate the skin, nose and eyes.

Draughtproofing

● **If you can see light around a door or window,** or hear whistling, air is getting in and out. To find less obvious leaks, hold a wet hand in front of doors, windows and other openings. You'll feel any draught on your damp hand.

● **Draughtproof doors and windows with foam strips** or permanent mouldings. Use a permanent draught excluder or 'door sausage' to seal a gap under a door.

● **Seal narrow gaps with foam seals or mouldings** or use a liquid caulking compound. Latex and silicone-based sealants are the least toxic.

● **Window panes cause up to 20 per cent of heat loss** in winter, so make sure you cover windows with thick curtains and a pelmet and consider installing double-glazing, which can cut heat loss by 50 per cent.

PAY LESS

You'll be surprised at the difference effective insulation can make to your energy bills:

● Insulating the roof and ceiling will save you between 20 and 40 per cent of heating costs.

● Insulating the walls can cut the same costs by another 10 per cent or more.

● Insulate the floor and you could reduce the same costs by between 5 and 10 per cent.

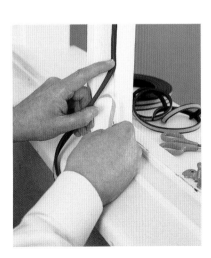

Seal any gaps round windows and doors. Draughtproofing can cut heat loss by up to 25 per cent in winter.

Warming solutions

How efficiently you heat your home will have a major impact on your fuel bills and your comfort. Think carefully about how you are using – and losing – heat. Good insulation (see page 12) is essential for energy efficiency, but there are other important steps to take.

First steps

● **On sunny days in winter,** open up the house to the south to let in the sun's warmth.

● **Close doors between heated and unheated areas** to keep the warmth in the area you are heating.

● **Minimise heat escape through doors and windows.** Replace any cracked window panes. Draw curtains at dusk. Cover windows with thick curtains and pelmets.

● **Consider double glazing,** especially if your windows need replacing. Two layers of glass instead of one in a window, with a layer of air trapped between, act as an insulator and reduce down-draughts. Installations must be carried out by a FENSA (Fenestration Self-Assessment) registered company. See also box, right.

● **Position heaters away from windows** to avoid unnecessary heat loss.

● **Don't heat empty rooms.** Unoccupied rooms only need to be heated occasionally to keep damp at bay.

● **Don't hang full-length curtains over a radiator.** When closed, they trap the heat between the curtain and window. Choose curtains that stop just below the window sill.

● **Before you turn up the heating,** think about putting on another layer of clothing instead.

● **Remember to turn off the heating** before leaving your home unoccupied for any length of time, and turn it off or to low before you go to bed.

● **In gas fires, dust can block air intakes,** causing faulty combustion and emission of toxic fumes, including carbon monoxide. If you notice a gas flame burning orange or yellow rather than blue, have your heater serviced.

Energy-efficient heating options

● **Select an appropriate boiler for your needs.** Consider whether it will be supplying heating and hot water, the size of your family and how many bathrooms it will service.

LOW-EMISSIVITY GLASS

Low-emissivity (Low-E) glass has a virtually invisible ultra-thin coating on one side. When used to form the inner pane of a double glazing unit, it reflects heat back into the building and also allows the sun's energy to pass into the room. This makes Low-E glass as energy-efficient as triple glazing, but without the 50 per cent weight increase and the extra thickness that is involved.

Every 1°C increase in thermostat temperature can increase your energy bill by 10 per cent or more

......heating limits......

Try to limit the area you need to heat. If you can halve the area, you'll halve your heating costs.

• **Switch to a high-efficiency boiler.** If your boiler is more than 15 years old it's probably time to replace it. By law, all new boilers in England and Wales must be high-efficiency condensing boilers. These can save up to one-third on heating bills and you should recoup the cost of the boiler in reduced fuel bills after four years. There are two types: regular, which heat water through a hot water cylinder; and combination ('combi') boilers, which supply instant hot water without the need for a cylinder. Condensing boilers can easily be fitted to most new and old heating systems. Always use a registered qualified installer.

• **Install thermostatic radiator valves.** These valves reduce the flow of water through the radiators to which they are fitted, opening and closing according to the temperature in the room. They save money and energy by allowing you to control individual room temperatures.

• **Update your central heating programmer.** Modern programmers are much more efficient as they are designed to ensure that the boiler works only when it is needed.

• **Use a boiler energy manager** to make sure your boiler works only when it is needed. These sophisticated devices reduce wasteful 'short cycling' on a boiler – that is, when 'hot water only' is selected on a conventional central heating programmer, the boiler switches on and off continually to keep the water in the boiler at the selected temperature, even though the cylinder is already full of hot water. This 'short cycling' can add as much as 30 per cent to fuel bills.

• **Ensure your radiators are the right size.** If they are too large for the room you will be heating extra water to fill them, then turning them down because the room is too hot.

• **Have all heating appliances serviced regularly** to ensure that they are operating efficiently.

For maximum efficiency, opt for individual thermostatic radiator valves (TRVs). They allow you to control the temperature in each room.

WOOD FIRES

Burning wood is an eco-friendly choice if the wood is from a sustainable source. Install wood-burning stoves, which are the most efficient fires and can also be used to heat water.

• Make sure your wood comes from a sustainable source. Check with the Forest Stewardship Council.

• Ensure you use only clean, high-quality wood that has been dried, or 'seasoned', for at least a year. This will help to minimise air pollution.

• Don't collect firewood from parks as it provides vital habitat and nesting material for animals.

• Never burn any wood that has been coated with varnish, paint or other chemicals as it could emit toxic fumes.

• Don't let logs smoulder for long periods, such as overnight, as this increases the output of pollutants.

• Always remember to get your chimney checked and cleaned once a year by a professional chimney cleaner to ensure that it is working efficiently.

• When you are removing excess wood ash from the fire grate add it to your compost – it is an excellent source of potassium, which promotes healthy plant growth.

Switched-on lighting

Lighting is one of your household energy costs that can easily be cut – by more than half, if you're careful. Start by opening up your house to nature's free and highly efficient light source, the sun. Then look at adopting low-energy, long-life technologies.

Natural lighting

● **Maximising your use of natural light** will save on lighting bills, warm your home and help to eliminate germs and dust mites.

● **Paint interior walls in pale shades** and use mirrors to reflect natural light, particularly in dark rooms.

● **On bright, sunny days open blinds and curtains** to admit as much light as possible.

● **Consider installing skylights in dark corners** such as hallways or small rooms with no windows. To minimise heat loss, make sure they are covered at night.

● **A cheap and effective alternative to a skylight** is a sunlight pipe. Known as Sola-vent, the system consists of a sun pipe, solar-powered fan and two low voltage 50W halogen lights, all housed in one unit. It concentrates and reflects natural light through a diffuser into the room below and also provides solar-powered ventilation.

Which kind of lighting?

Aesthetics are important when it comes to lighting, but choosing the right light for each location is just as crucial. An appropriate, efficient light will not only increase comfort, it will also save energy and reduce long-term costs.

● **Conventional incandescent light bulbs** are inefficient because most of the energy used to run them is turned into heat rather than light. Although cheap to buy, they have to be replaced regularly. Limit your use of incandescent bulbs to areas where you need light instantly and only for a short time, such as a bathroom or under-stairs cupboard. These bulbs will be phased out by 2011.

● **Consider using halogen bulbs,** which throw a bright light similar to natural light, to illuminate a work area or to spotlight a painting. They are expensive to buy, but usually last about twice as long as conventional light bulbs.

Natural light is free and abundant. Make the most of it in your home and position work areas, such as a desk or kitchen sink, close to a window where possible.

TYPES OF ARTIFICIAL LIGHTING

Lighting type	Purchase costs	Life span (hours)	Running costs	Energy use
Fluorescent	Medium	6,000-15,000	Low	Low
Halogen	Medium	2,000-4,000	Medium	Medium
Incandescent	Low	1,000-2,500	High	High

SMART LIGHTING

- Select the lowest acceptable wattage for all lights. More watts mean you use more power.

- Turn lights off whenever you leave a room, but avoid very frequent switching on and off of low-energy bulbs as this shortens their lifespan.

- Use low-wattage lights for general room lighting, saving more powerful lights for places where you do close work.

- A low-wattage light close to where it is needed is more efficient than using a stronger light placed further away.

- Lights with multiple bulbs are inefficient: about six 25-watt bulbs are needed to match one 100-watt bulb's output.

- Don't install light fittings that obscure the light.

- Use timers or light or heat sensors to control your outside lights or use solar-powered garden lights.

- Install contact switches in cupboards so that lights go on when you open the door and off when you close it.

- A dimmer switch normally set to dimmed uses more energy than a lower-wattage bulb with an on/off switch.

● **Think twice before installing halogen downlighting.** These lights throw hard-edged spotlights rather than ambient light, so it takes up to six of them to light the same area as a single incandescent bulb.

● **Remember that low-voltage halogen lights** need transformers, so you'll need to fit downlight transformers in your roof cavity.

● **Consider using LEDs** (light emitting diodes) as a light source. These last virtually for ever, they don't emit heat and they consume very little electricity.

Low energy lighting

Energy-saving fluorescent lightbulbs consume about one quarter of the energy of equivalent incandescent bulbs and last around 10 times longer. They are available in two forms: traditional tube lights, which are cheaper but require special fittings, and compact fluorescent lamps (CFLs), which fit standard light sockets.

● **Use fluorescent lights** where you need light for long periods – for example in kitchens or living areas.

● **Next time you need to replace a conventional light** bulb, try an energy-saving light bulb, then gradually replace all incandescent bulbs in high-use areas.

● **Generally, it's wise to buy a slightly higher wattage** for energy-saving light bulbs than is usually recommended by the manufacturer because they may dim a little over time.

● **Look for energy-saving bulbs that come in two pieces,** a fitting and a bulb. That allows you to replace just the bulb rather than the whole unit.

Low-energy compact fluorescent bulbs pay for themselves in savings after 18 months and at least twice again in their lifespan.

Heating water

The average household uses 220-320 litres of hot water a day, so it is worth taking time to find the best and most efficient ways of heating and using your supply.

Hot water savers

● **Check that your hot-water cylinder is the right size for your requirements** and is properly insulated.

● **Think before turning on the hot water.** Will cold water suffice – for example, for rinsing dishes and washing clothes? This simple step can save up to 25 per cent of your water-heating bill.

● **Keep your thermostat setting fairly low** – about 60°C (but over 55°C to kill off bacteria). Having the water too hot is a waste of energy and means that you use more cold water to make it cooler. Lowering the temperature also reduces the risk of scalds.

● **Fix a dripping hot tap.** It could be wasting up to 10 bathtubs full of hot water a month.

● **Avoid using hot water in short spurts** throughout the day. Instead, do several jobs that need hot water at once. This way, less water is left in the pipes to go cold.

● **Consider the pros and cons of taking a shower or a bath.** See page 28.

● **Install a water-efficient showerhead** and cut hot-water usage by up to half.

● **Install tap aerators and flow restrictors.** These limit the flow without reducing pressure.

● **Heat water only as needed.** Switch on an immersion heater or the boiler only about an hour before hot water is required, and switch it off again when it is not wanted.

● **Use eco-kettles for boiling water.** They will heat only the precise amount of water you need and consume a third of the energy used by a standard kettle.

Washing clothes in cold water can cut the greenhouse gas output *of your* washing machine *by a factor of fifteen*

Check that all pipes and tanks are fully lagged. Reheating water that has gone cold can account for up to half your hot water bill.

..... **running cold** ....
When you run a hot tap, 4 litres of cold water can be wasted before the water runs hot. Use cold water whenever possible.

Solar heating

Generating heat for a hot-water system through solar panels is an efficient option for most homes. The conventional hot-water system is kept as a back-up but you may be amazed at how little you need to use it. Although the set-up costs are high, a solar water heating system used together with a gas-powered back-up should pay for itself in energy savings in 10 to 15 years. The payback time may be faster if your old water-heating system was very expensive to run.

● **Solar heating can supply at least 50 per cent of your household's hot water requirements** over the course of a year and as much as 90 per cent in the summer.

● **Vacuum-tube or evacuated tube systems are more efficient** than the cheaper flat-plate options and work even on a cloudy, overcast day.

● **Make sure your roof is strong enough to support the system** – the panels are often very heavy.

● **Place the hot water storage tank as close as possible to the solar panels** in order to minimise heat loss from connecting pipes.

● **Avoid drawing off large quantities of hot water late in the afternoon and evening** as there will be little sunlight to heat the replenished tank of water and you will be more likely to need a boost of heating from your conventional source.

● **Shower or take baths in the morning** so the sun can heat the replacement water during the day and the insulated tank will keep it warm until it is required the next morning.

● **Set the thermostat on the booster to a maximum of 60°C.** The lower the setting, the lower the amount of energy needed to supplement the solar heating.

A sunny, south-facing pitched roof allows solar panels to catch the maximum sunlight throughout the day.

SOLAR OPTIONS

There are two types of solar heating:

● Solar collectors absorb energy from the sun and use it to heat water.

● Photovoltaic, or solar panels, transform the energy captured from sunlight directly into electricity.

Using water wisely

By adopting water-conscious habits, it's possible to halve your water consumption. You'll be helping reduce pressure on limited water supplies, protecting the environment by reducing your sewerage outputs and saving money at the same time.

Top ten water-saving tips

1 **If you have a leaking tap, fix it at once** – it could be wasting as much as 2,000 litres of water a month. Don't keep tightening the tap as this will wear the washer and make the leak worse.

2 **A running tap can waste 15 litres of water a minute,** so always turn it off when shaving or brushing your teeth. Whenever you are waiting for cold water to run hot, collect the cold water in a jug or bucket and then use it – for watering indoor plants, filling the kettle, or any other purpose. You could save up to 4 litres of water each time.

3 **Take shorter showers or shallower baths** (see box, page 28). Every minute less spent in the shower can save up to 23 litres of water, depending on the efficiency of your showerhead, so get into the habit of turning off the shower while shampooing your hair.

A water-efficient washing machine can save more than 100 litres of water per wash

HOW MUCH WATER DO YOU USE?

Being aware of how much water your individual household appliances use will help you to identify opportunities for making water savings. Do what you can to cut down on unnecessary usage of water and consider changing your habits, for example, to take showers instead of baths. When replacing appliances such as washing machines and dishwashers, look for energy-efficient models and ones that tailor their use to the needs of each wash. This chart lists the average water usage for the most common appliances and household tasks.

WC	Water usage	Dishwashing	Water usage
Standard full flush	11 litres	By hand	18 litres
Standard half flush	5.5 litres	Standard machine	36 litres
Efficient full flush	6 litres	Efficient machine	16 litres
Efficient half flush	3 litres		
Shower	**Water usage**	**Clothes washing**	**Water usage**
Standard shower head	Up to 23 litres/minute	Standard machine	200 litres
Water-saving shower head	9 litres/minute	Efficient machine	100 litres
		Most efficient	50 litres
Bath	**Water usage**	**Outdoors**	**Water usage**
Shallow bath	50 litres	Garden sprinkler	1,000 litres/hour
Full bath	150 litres	Washing car with hose	17 litres/minute
General use	**Water usage**	Washing car using bucket	30 litres
Washing, brushing teeth, etc	18 litres per person/day		

Each time you wash vegetables in a bowl of water rather than under a running tap you could save about 30 litres.

4 **If you have one, use the half-flush option on your toilet** when appropriate, to save about 8 litres per flush.

5 **Don't run your washing machine until you have a full load.** Reducing the number of washes you do can save huge amounts of water – some top-loading washing machines can use as much as 240 litres per wash.

6 **Use your dishwasher only when it is full.** You can save up to 50 litres for every wash you don't do.

7 **If you are washing dishes by hand,** rinse them in a sink full of cold water rather than under a running tap – which could use 15 litres a minute.

8 **Use a water meter to help monitor your water consumption.** If you don't have a water meter, phone your water supplier to get one fitted.

9 **When washing the car, use a bucket and sponge** rather than a hose. If you use buckets you'll save more than 150 litres per wash.

10 To clean driveways, paths and paved areas, sweep them with a broom instead of hosing.

FIX THAT LEAK

Small leaks can waste huge amounts of water. If your water is metered, from time to time run this check for a leaking pipe.
  Turn off all taps and machines that use water. Write down the water meter reading. Check it again half an hour later. If it has gone up, you have a leak. Call a plumber if you can't find the leak yourself.

.....**dishwasher savvy**...........
  When **stacking the dishwasher,**
scrape off excess food rather than rinsing
plates under a running tap.

Water-saving hardware

Many accessories and fittings are designed to save water.

● **Replace separate taps with a single-lever mixer tap.** This will help you to adjust the water temperature more rapidly, thereby saving water.

● **Consider updating your taps and showerheads** to the latest models which incorporate aeration devices. These mix air with the water to reduce the flow without losing pressure. They are sometimes called champagne showerheads as they put bubbles into the water. Switching to these showerheads can save up to 50,000 litres of water a year, without you really noticing a difference.

● **Update your cistern to a high-efficiency dual flush system.** This gives you the option of choosing a half or full flush and can reduce flush volume from 11 litres to 3 litres.

● **If you have a conventional cistern,** you could install a commercially available flush regulator known as a 'Hippo'. This will save 3 litres per flush in a 9-litre cistern. For a low-tech option, put a large plastic bottle of water in the cistern, well clear of the flush mechanism – a 3-litre bottle will save 3 litres per flush. Or simply adjust (or carefully bend) the float arm so that it closes the valve at a lower water level.

Water-saving in the garden

However parched your lawn looks during a period of drought, don't breach a hosepipe ban and water it. Watering the lawn is usually an unnecessary waste of water and the grass will return to its lush green as soon as it rains.

● **Gradually reduce how often you water the garden** to encourage plants to put down strong, deep roots.

● **Soak plants thoroughly but infrequently** rather than watering little and often.

● **Don't water the garden during the heat of the day;** instead water in the cool of the evening or in the early morning to reduce evaporation.

● **Even when water restrictions aren't in force,** use minimal water on the lawn. Increase drought-resistance of grass by not cutting it too short (about 3cm is ideal); by aerating it occasionally with a garden fork to improve water penetration; and by not over-fertilising – the more fertiliser you use, the more water you need to keep the grass lush.

...... water watch ....

An A-rated water-saving washing machine monitors the size of the wash and uses only as much water as is required.

Fit a water butt – preferably made of recycled plastic – to collect free rainwater from a downpipe. Opt for the largest size you can accommodate.

● **Use water butts to collect as much rainwater** as possible and use this to water your lawn, flowerbeds and containers. Pure rainwater is actually better for your plants than treated tap water and in hot weather is warmer so less of a shock to your plants. When wet weather is forecast, leave empty watering cans outside to fill with rainwater.

● **Fit a trigger nozzle to hosepipes** so you can deliver water only where it is needed rather than spraying wastefully around the garden, and repair any leaks in hosepipes.

● **Avoid using garden sprinklers,** which can use as much water in one hour as a family of four uses in an entire day. Many water companies will insist you have a meter installed if you intend to use a sprinkler.

COLLECTING AND USING GREY WATER

Grey water is the waste water from baths, showers, basins and washing machines. With some filtering, it can be recycled for watering the garden, washing the car, flushing the toilet and other jobs where the quality of the water is not critical.

● A pump with a hosepipe attachment can be bought which will empty bathwater directly on to the garden or into a collection tank via an open window.

● Water from washing dishes is not suitable as it will contain grease and food waste that will encourage bacteria to grow in the tank.

● Grey water should not be stored for longer than 24 hours as it can contain bacteria that may breed, so it is not suitable for collecting in large tanks that will not be emptied on a regular basis.

● Keep children and pets away from grey water.

● Never put grey water on fruit and vegetables that may be eaten raw.

● Restrict the use of untreated grey water to the garden. Use only treated grey water to flush the toilet and wash clothes.

Room by room

Different strategies are required to make each part of your home energy-efficient, comfortable and healthy and as eco-friendly as possible.

The efficient kitchen

Our kitchens are big energy and water users and they are the main source of household waste, so it's well worth taking the time to evaluate your kitchen routines and to make some changes. Using resources wisely, running energy-efficient appliances and recycling will pay dividends for you, your home and the environment.

Ten cool savers

1 **Fridges and freezers are energy-hungry** appliances, so when buying choose high-efficiency models.

2 **Don't be tempted to keep an old fridge running** as a back-up unless you really need it. It's likely to be more energy-hungry than newer, more energy-efficient models.

3 **Locate your fridge in a cool spot,** away from heat-producing appliances, with an air space of at least 8cm around the coils at the back. A lack of space or ventilation can reduce efficiency by as much as 15 per cent.

4 **Don't set the thermostat too cold.** The ideal temperature for a fridge is 3 to 4°C; for a freezer it's -18 to -15°C. Every 1°C reduction can increase energy use by 5 per cent.

5 **Open the door as little as possible.** For every minute it is open, it will take the fridge 3 minutes to cool down again.

6 **Keep the fridge at least two-thirds full.** Food retains cold better than air does.

7 **Regularly check the door seals** by closing the door over a piece of paper; if you can pull the paper out easily, the seal isn't strong enough. Tighten the hinges or replace the seals. (You can use this method to check oven seals, too.)

8 **Defrost the freezer every 3 months** if it's not a frost-free model. Never let more than 5mm of frost accumulate in the freezer.

9 **Clean the coils at the back annually** to keep the appliance working efficiently.

10 **Before going away for a long period,** empty the fridge, turn it off and leave the door open or ajar.

GREENFREEZE

Until the late 1980s, the main coolants used in fridges were chlorofluorocarbons (CFCs). These damaged the ozone layer and were banned. CFCs were then replaced with hydrofluorocarbons (HFCs) and hydrochlorofluorocarbons (HCFCs). Unfortunately these were also found to damage the ozone and, in the case of HFCs, increase global warming.

Greenpeace developed an ozone-friendly cooling technology. Known as Greenfreeze, it uses natural hydrocarbons. More than 100 million Greenfreeze appliances have been sold worldwide. Many major brands have Greenfreeze models; ask your supplier for details.

Switch from electricity to gas for cooking and **cut annual household greenhouse gas** output by half a tonne

Stove sense

When buying cooking appliances, check energy ratings and use the following to help you make an eco-friendly choice.

● **If possible, choose gas** for cooking. Gas hobs cost half as much to run as electric ones and yield half the amount of greenhouse gases.

● **Don't buy anything larger than you need.** In general, the larger the stove, the more energy it will use.

● **Choose a hob with a range of ring sizes.** This will help you to control energy use.

● **On an electric stove top coil hotplates** tend to be cheaper and more efficient than solid or ceramic hotplates.

● **If you opt for electricity,** consider induction hotplates. These are up to 30 per cent more efficient than standard hotplates. A pan placed on the hotplate creates a magnetic field, causing the pan, but not the hob, to heat up. Little energy is wasted, and temperature control is precise.

A good layout is the first step towards an efficient kitchen. Never buy a bigger appliance than you need. A gas hob and electric fan-assisted oven are often an energy-efficient solution.

Cost-effective cooking

● **Use a microwave for small dishes and reheating.** Microwaves use less energy and generate much lower greenhouse emissions than hobs.

● **Invest in a pressure cooker.** It will cook the food in a third of the time required by a conventional hob, using one-third as much energy.

● **To reduce the cooking time of frozen foods,** thaw them thoroughly in the fridge before cooking.

● **Match the size of your pan to the hotplate,** and keep the flame as low as possible. If the flame extends beyond the edge of the saucepan base, you are wasting energy.

● **Cooking one small dish in an oven is inefficient.** If you are using the oven, try to cook several dishes at once.

● **Try not to open the oven door** when cooking. The oven loses about 15°C of heat each time you do so.

Choosing and using a dishwasher

A major consumer of water and energy in the kitchen is an automatic dishwasher. Dishwashers can, however, be quite efficient if you select the right model and use it wisely.

● **When buying a dishwasher,** choose one with a high energy rating.

● **Choose a model with a wide range of settings,** including an economy setting, to give you more options for saving energy. Use the economy setting whenever possible.

● **Look for models that have a half-load option.** Some have two drawers that can be used separately or together. Using a half-load can save over 9 litres of water per wash.

● **Consider buying a model that can be run on cold water.** When hot water is required, the machine heats it, generally using less energy than a conventional water heater. Otherwise, always choose a cycle with a cold rinse, if that is available.

● **When buying a dishwasher,** choose one that permits 'no-heat' or air-drying. If your dishwasher does have a heat-drying function, turn it off and let the dishes air-dry. This can reduce energy use by more than 10 per cent.

● **For maximum efficiency** follow the manufacturer's instructions for loading dishes and selecting programs.

● **Rather than rinsing plates before you put them in the machine,** which can double your water use, simply scrape any excess food into your garbage bin. Most modern dishwashing machines will be able to filter the rest.

SIMPLE WATER SAVERS

We use about 8 per cent of our annual domestic water supply in the kitchen. The following tips will help you to cut consumption.

● If you have one of the old-model dishwashers, make a habit of washing small amounts of dishes by hand.

● When washing dishes by hand, rinse them in a second sink or basin filled with cold water rather than under a running tap.

● Wash fruit and vegetables in a basin or bowl of water rather than under a running tap. Reuse the water afterwards by pouring it on your lawn or plants.

fan power

Choose an oven with a fan. Up to 25% more efficient than a conventional oven, it produces up to 35% less greenhouse gas.

• **Use the dishwasher only when it is fully loaded.**

• **If your dishwasher uses hot water** and you have an off-peak hot water option, run the dishwasher at night when it will cost less.

• **Clean the filter regularly** for optimal operation.

• **To avoid the chemical pollutants contained in many dishwashing products** use environmentally friendly, preferably plant-based, alternatives.

Waste not

• **Try to reduce the amount of food packaging you bring home.** Buy fruit and vegetables loose and remember to take your own bags when you go food shopping.

• **Reuse packaging as much as possible.** Bottles, jars and plastic containers can be washed and reused time and time again.

• **Recycle as much of your rubbish as possible,** but follow your local council guidelines (see pages 90-93).

• **Don't put food scraps down the toilet or sink.** Instead, recycle them using a garden compost heap or, if space is tight, a worm farm (see page 113).

• **Put a strainer in your sink plughole** to catch food scraps, then add them to the compost.

• **Avoid using sink waste-disposal units** as these use extra water and flush food scraps into waste pipes.

DISHWASHER OR SINK?

Washing dishes in the sink certainly saves energy and, if you are careful not to waste water while rinsing, it can be the best option in terms of water use, too. But if you have a modern, high-efficiency dishwasher and use it correctly – running a full load on an economy setting – you may use just 16 litres of water each time. That's 2 litres less than the average hand wash uses. In comparison, an older (1980s), low-efficiency dishwasher is likely to use about 36 litres of water.

Always wait until your washing machine and dishwasher are full before switching them on: washing two half loads uses more water – and energy – than one full load.

The water-wise bathroom

The bathroom is where we use the largest amount of water, but it's also where we can make the greatest contribution to conserving this valuable resource.

Send less down the drain

● **Fit a water-saving champagne showerhead.** This can reduce water output by at least 9 litres a minute.

● **Take shorter showers.** Every minute less can save as much as 23 litres of water (see box, right).

● **When waiting for a shower to run hot,** catch the cold water in a bucket to use on your indoor plants or in the garden. Keep a container handy at the basin, too.

● **Having a bath often uses more water** than taking a shower (see box, right), so don't overfill the bath: add just enough water to cover yourself when lying down.

● **Consider installing a grey water system** to recycle water from the bath, shower and basin (see Collecting and using grey water, page 23).

● **Install aerating taps.** These reduce water flow by up to 50 per cent, saving up to 5,000 litres a year.

● **Consider a single-lever mixing tap:** it will help you to obtain the right water temperature more quickly.

● **When you turn on the taps,** don't turn them on full blast – up to 90 per cent of the water may be wasted. Get into the habit of releasing just as much as you need.

● **Don't leave the tap running** when you are brushing your teeth. A running tap can waste as much as 15 litres of water a minute.

● **When shaving,** rinse your razor in a cup of water instead of under a running tap or in a sink of water.

Toilet training

● **When buying a new toilet,** choose a model with a water-efficient model.

● **Fit an efficient dual-flush toilet.** The half-flush option can save 8 litres of water per flush.

● **If you don't have a dual-flush toilet,** a simple water-saving device placed in the cistern will reduce its water usage (see page 22).

● **Think before you flush.** Consider whether you really need to flush each time you use the toilet. Fewer flushes can soon add up to considerable water savings.

● **Consider installing a water-free toilet.** A composting toilet uses no water at all. Instead, the waste works its way slowly through a large tank below the floor. By the time it reaches the bottom of the tank it has degraded into manure that can be used on your garden.

Pros & cons

Bath or shower?
A bath is generally assumed to use far more water than a shower, but it depends on the efficiency of your shower and how frugal you are in the bath. A shallow bath uses about 50 litres of water, whereas a full one may consume 150 litres. An inefficient showerhead can use up to 23 litres a minute; so, within just over 2 minutes, you'll have used as much as a shallow bath and if you shower for 7 minutes, you'll have used more than a full bath. In contrast, an efficient showerhead uses only 9 litres a minute, so a 3 or 4-minute shower will consume significantly less than a shalllow bath.

The green utility room

Try to minimise your energy consumption when doing the laundry, and whenever possible use cold water. Eco-friendly soaps and powders cost no more than chemical detergents, are kind to fabrics and are better for the garden if you want to reuse the water.

Washing sense

● **Wait until you have a full load** before running your washing machine. If you have to do a smaller wash, remember to reset the water level.

● **Stick to a short cycle,** which is usually sufficient for all but heavily soiled items.

● **Don't use more detergent than you need.** It won't make the clothes any cleaner, they will be more difficult to rinse properly and you will waste soap and energy – for every 100g of detergent that is produced, about 1.3kg of greenhouse gases are emitted.

● **Use eco-friendly detergents and soaps** that are petrochemical and phosphate-free or low in phosphate. Choose concentrated forms: they don't contain bulking agents, are cheaper and need less packaging.

● **Soap nuts are a natural washing detergent.** The fruit of the Soap nut tree, they contain the natural active washing ingredient saponin. Put 6-8 nuts in the bag provided, place in the washing machine with your laundry and wash as usual. Reuse the bag three times, then compost the nuts and keep the sack to use again.

● **Choose the most efficient model of washing machine** you can find. Washing machines carry ratings for energy and water efficiency.

Dry wisely

● **Whenever possible, hang washing outside to dry.** Sunlight helps to eliminate bacteria and dust mites. In bad weather use a drying rack indoors rather than a dryer.

● **Shake and smooth out clothes** before hanging them, to reduce the need for ironing.

● **A tumble dryer is energy-hungry.** If you need to use it, switch it to a medium setting rather than high.

● **Do separate loads of heavy and light items,** as mixing them will increase the drying time.

● **Use the washing machine spin cycle to dry clothes** as much as possible before putting them in the dryer: this can cut greenhouse emissions by as much as 2kg per load.

If you have off-peak electricity, run your machine at night and you will save money

Clean the filter regularly to keep your washing machine working efficiently. After each tumble dryer load clean the filter to prevent it clogging and posing a fire hazard.

..... cold is cool ....
Washing your clothes in cold water uses approximately 90 per cent less energy than if you use hot water.

SLEEP RIGHT

● Keep bedroom furniture to a minimum so that you can dust and vacuum easily and regularly.

● Buy furniture made of wood from a sustainable source varnished with eco-friendly products.

● Open the windows each day to refresh the air.

● Pull back the covers each morning to air the sheets for a few hours, and hang bedding out to air from time to time.

● When you change the sheets, let the mattress air for a while. To minimise dust mites, vacuum the mattress every six months.

● If dust or dust mites are still a problem, remove carpets, heavy curtains, padded head boards and cushions. Consider storing clothes in another room.

● Minimise the number of electrical appliances in your bedroom to reduce your exposure to electromagnetic fields.

The natural bedroom

We spend about a third of our lives in the bedroom, so it pays to make it as healthy a place as possible. Investing in quality beds and bedding may cost more, but will increase comfort, contribute to good health and protect resources. It will also save you money in the long run, as quality products last longer.

Which bed?

Many of the beds and most of the mattresses we buy incorporate synthetic materials. These materials are derived from non-renewable petrochemicals, can contain volatile organic compounds (VOCs) that emit harmful fumes (see page 75) and are seldom recyclable.

● **When selecting your bed base,** opt for one made of natural materials, preferably wood from a sustainable source, and sealed with non-toxic, biodegradable stains or varnishes. Bases made of wood composites are often made with adhesives containing VOCs.

● **When buying a mattress,** consider one made of natural, biodegradable materials such as cotton, wool or natural latex (harvested sustainably from rubber trees).

● **As a long-term investment,** consider a pure latex mattress – many are guaranteed for 10 years and can last up to 25 years. Latex is light and offers good support. It is also less likely to harbour dust mites than other materials, is naturally antibacterial and resistant to moisture build-up. Check with the maker that no chemicals have been added.

● **Cotton and wool mattresses** are reasonably priced, comfortable, durable and allow good air circulation; wool is also an effective heat regulator. They do, however, require regular airing in the sun, to avoid compaction and to keep moisture retention and dust mites to a minimum, and are often heavy and difficult to manoeuvre. Check with the manufacturers that no chemicals have been added.

● **Good-quality sprung mattresses,** widely available at reasonable prices, offer good back support and last 10 years or more. But many contain synthetic materials, such as polyurethane foams, which may emit chemical fumes.

● **If you opt for a mattress made of synthetic materials,** ask the manufacturer if potentially harmful chemicals, such as flame retardants, have been used in production.

● **If you buy beds and bedding** that contain VOCs, leave them in a well-ventilated space for a fortnight before use, then air them regularly. Fumes will diminish over time.

latex luxury

Natural, light, supportive and antibacterial, latex mattresses don't harbour dust mites and can last 25 years.

Greener bedding

- **Choose bed linen made of natural fibres** derived from environmentally friendly sources.

- **Consider wool blankets instead of a duvet.** Heavy duvets often make us too hot, resulting in disturbed sleep patterns. Using three or four blankets allows you to adjust the covering to suit the temperature.

- **Opt for natural fillings,** such as cotton or down, rather than synthetics, when buying pillows or a duvet.

- **Cover your mattress with a protector made of natural fibres,** such as wool or cotton. This will help to absorb sweat, protect you from dust mites in the mattress and can make an old mattress feel more comfortable.

BEDDING AND THE ENVIRONMENT

COTTON Inexpensive, comfortable, lets air circulate, wears well. Conventional production uses large amounts of water as well as fertilisers, pesticides and bleaches. Requires large doses of chemicals to absorb dyes. The darker the colour, the more chemicals are used for the dye.

ORGANIC COTTON Same qualities as conventional cotton, but produced without chemicals and dyes. End product is therefore safer, but more expensive.

DUCK AND GOOSE DOWN Natural, soft, light. Effective heat and moisture regulator. Generally a by-product of breeding ducks for food. Moderately expensive.

HEMP Strong, breathes well, naturally hypoallergenic and antibacterial. Production requires relatively little water and few or no pesticides. Absorbs dyes easily without chemical additives. Not yet widely available; moderately expensive.

POLYESTER Inexpensive, easy to maintain, but doesn't breathe well. Derived from non-renewable petroleum; production yields toxic waste. May contain VOCs.

WOOL Renewable, plentiful. Effective heat and moisture regulator, naturally flame retardant. May contain pesticide residues, and dyed and treated wool may contain chemicals. Moderately expensive.

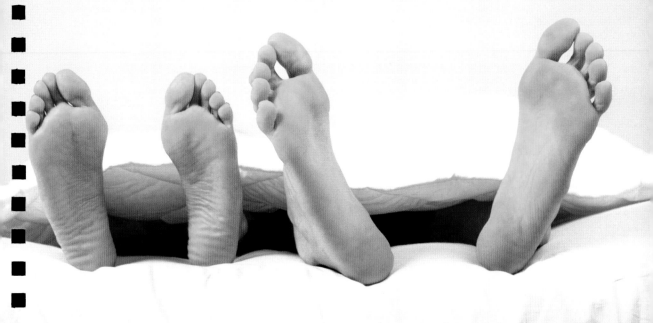

Buy bedding made from **organic wool.** It's durable, soft, warm **and free from allergens**

Your baby's needs are natural and simple so let the nursery reflect that. Secondhand bargains are often the wisest investments.

Mother nature's nursery

If there's a baby on the way, think carefully before you spend a small fortune on items you'll need for only a few months. If you take account of your family's impact on the environment when they're still babies, then you'll establish habits to last you – and them – a lifetime.

Baby kit

There is something irresistible about baby furniture and accessories. But before you run up a huge store-card bill, stop and think. Your baby will thrive even if you don't splash out on coordinated rugs, pictures, sleeping bags, cot bumpers and curtains. So what's the answer?

● **Larger pieces of equipment,** including prams, cots, playpens and highchairs are sturdily constructed and designed to last, so why not buy them secondhand? You can find great bargains online through eBay or in the small ads of the local paper, while most local National Childbirth Trust branches hold regular nearly-new sales.

● **Baby linens** – blankets, sheets, towels and so forth – can all be borrowed or bought secondhand.

● **Instead of buying stacks of sheets for the crib** or moses basket, cut down those much loved and wonderfully soft, but thinning, cotton sheets that you've been meaning to replace for months. One double sheet can be cut down to make half-a-dozen crib sheets.

● **For daytime naps, you need light-excluding curtains.** Charity shops often have beautifully made nursery curtains. You can interline flimsy curtains with old blankets to help to exclude both light and draughts.

● **Cotton cellular blankets** are ideal for layering in cots; if you buy these new, choose organic cotton (see opposite).

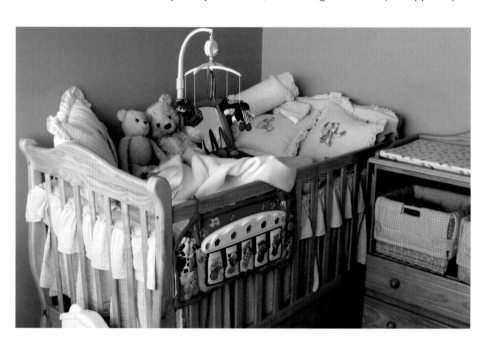

make it yourself

Make your own mobile
Watching a mobile moving above the cot or pram will help your baby's eyes to co-ordinate and brain to grow. Remember, newborn babies can only see things 15-20cm away, and until the age of 6 months, babies respond best to black-and-white or other bold contrasting colours. All you need to make a mobile is a coat hanger, some string and a selection of interesting objects. You could use Christmas baubles, lightly crumpled tinfoil, a balloon (draw a smiling face on the side your baby can see in thick marker pen), lengths of coloured ribbon that will move in the slightest draught, small, lightweight stuffed toys or pompoms. There are no limits – everything fascinates a baby. Attach several items to the hanger using thin string (dental floss works well), adjust them until the mobile balances and then hang it securely from a hook in the ceiling.

Replace the items frequently to stimulate your baby, and remember to make sure that, as your baby grows, he or she can't reach the mobile.

The bottom end

The average child gets through 5,000 disposable nappies from birth to potty training – nappies that take hundreds of years to rot down in landfill sites. Here are several good reasons for using modern reusable nappies.

- **Modern cloth nappies** are easy to put on.

- **Washing is simple.** Drop dirty nappies into a lidded nappy bucket to soak. Your washing machine won't die from overuse: two or three nappy-washes a week, in an eco-friendly laundry detergent, should be enough.

- **Long-term savings.** Although expensive to buy, they work out far cheaper than disposables, and the environment benefits, too. A set of cloth nappies used by your baby can then be passed on to someone else. When worn out they can go into a fabric recycling bin.

What to wear...

Babies outgrow most outfits in three months or so. Here's how you can minimise waste and cost.

- **Borrow baby clothes.** Mother and baby groups are good places to meet people willing to share. Often, the more baby clothes are washed and worn, the softer they become.

- **Use charity shops.** The baby clothes have been nicely worn in, and the money you spend will go to a good cause.

- **Pass on clothes you no longer need,** to other parents or to charity shops.

- **If buying new baby clothes, consider organic cotton.** Though more expensive, the fabric is usually softer, and its chemical-free production is far less damaging to the environment and to the workers who produce it. Research suggests that around a quarter of the world's pesticides are used in conventional cotton farming, and that they account for thousands of deaths a year in developing countries.

BABYWIPES

Your baby's skin is a good deal thinner and more fragile than yours, making it far easier for chemicals to be absorbed into his or her bloodstream. One of the kindest things you can do – both for baby's bottom and for the environment – is to forgo the ubiquitous babywipe. These wipes are impregnated with all sorts of substances, often including preservatives and perfume.

Baby skin is too sensitive for this chemical cocktail. The wipes themselves are fairly indestructible, and often come in even more indestructible plastic boxes. It is much cheaper, kinder and more environmentally friendly to buy organic cotton wool or organic cotton flannels and wash with warm water.

Healthy living areas

Living areas aren't always the healthiest of places. We tend to sit in them for long periods, often with a heater on or watching television, possibly breathing in fumes from fittings and furniture. Ventilating the room and choosing natural materials and efficient appliances will protect health, enhance comfort and save money.

Natural comfort

● **Avoid furnishings and fittings made with synthetic products.** These often contain volatile organic compounds (VOCs), which emit harmful fumes (see page 74). Opt for natural, non-chemically treated furnishings and carpets.

● **Consider doing without carpets** – especially if any family members suffer from allergies or asthma – as they harbour dust mites and dirt.

● **Let sunlight and fresh air into living areas.** Warming and invigorating, sunlight also helps to eliminate dust mites. Open windows regularly to keep the area well ventilated.

● **Plants, such as rubber plants, help to clear the air** of chemical fumes (see Natural air filters, page 74).

● **In winter, heat the room efficiently** so that you are comfortable, but avoid overheating.

Good quality natural furnishings and flooring create a healthy living space. Make the most of natural light and limit the number of appliances.

Window coverings

● **Fit heavy, lined curtains.** These can cut heat loss by up to a third in winter. They should fit closely to the window, and extend beyond the bottom and sides of the frame.

● **Add a close-fitting box pelmet** to prevent draughts coming in over the top of the curtains.

Buying furniture

● **Buy for comfort and longevity** as well as for looks. Something that's the height of fashion is likely to be discarded after a few years and is less likely to be recycled.

● **Invest in good-quality furniture.** It may cost more initially, but is likely to last longer.

● **Choose natural materials** that come from sustainable sources and are biodegradable. Many of these, such as wood, are easier to repair than plastics or synthetics.

● **Avoid furniture made from synthetic foam** or composite wood products as these often contain VOCs, including formaldehyde, a probable carcinogen. Secondhand items are better in this respect as, over time, chemical emissions dwindle to insignificant levels.

● **Opt for wood that has been treated** with natural or low-toxicity oils, varnishes and stains.

● **Reject stain-repellent or fire-retardant treatments** as these chemicals can emit toxic fumes.

● **Look for labels that identify eco-friendly goods,** such as the Forest Stewardship Council trademark on furniture made from sustainable wood.

● **Recycle** unwanted goods whenever possible.

Home entertainment

● **Limit the number of appliances** in your living areas. Get rid of items you seldom use. Combination units, such as TV-DVD players, limit energy use and electromagnetic fields.

● **Choose products made by companies** that have agreed to eliminate toxic chemicals from production. Check manufacturers' websites for information.

● **Opt for energy-efficient models,** preferably bearing an energy-saving label, whenever possible.

● **Don't use standby mode: switch off appliances at the wall.** TVs, DVD players, stereos and computers are in standby mode for 60 per cent of their lifespan, and the power used by equipment standby can account for more than 10 per cent of household energy use.

NATURAL FURNISHINGS

Organic furnishing fabrics are manufactured from a range of natural fibres that are processed non-toxically: they include the obvious – cotton, wool, linen and silk – and the less familiar, derived from hemp, bamboo and even horsehair. Their disadvantage is their price; in many instances, saving the planet can cost you the earth.

Traditionally-made textiles in natural wool, such as tweed and tartan, are a good bet, and if you are looking for real durability, then consider leather upholstery – but watch out for synthetic stuffings.

By far the cheapest green alternative for textiles is to reuse and recycle. Charity shops, auctions, eBay and friends and relatives are all useful sources of secondhand curtains, rugs and other furnishing fabrics.

..... **secondhand gas** ....

Antique and secondhand furniture in original condition is less likely to emit harmful gases.

The home office

Most of us now have a computer at home and many have a home office. Even a small set-up can be a drain on energy and a cause of waste and pollution. So make sure you look after your resources and the environment.

Planning your office

● **Minimise clutter** so that you can easily dust, clean and access files, equipment and cables.

● **Make sure your office is well ventilated** as office equipment is a source of heat and unhealthy fumes.

● **Avoid furniture made from wood composites** as they contain volatile organic compounds (VOCs).

● **Consider buying secondhand furniture** to recycle materials, save money and reduce chemical fumes.

● **Maximise your use of natural light** by placing your desk near a window.

● **Use low-energy lightbulbs** for artificial lighting.

Buying equipment

● **Favour manufacturers with sound environmental policies.** Check their green credentials on the Internet.

● **Choose a computer** that can be upgraded easily.

● **Consider a laptop.** It can use up to 90 per cent less energy than a desktop machine, and can be easily hooked up to a monitor, keyboard and conventional mouse.

Selecting peripherals

● **To save energy, have peripherals,** such as CD drives, installed inside the computer rather than buying separate units, or buy units that are powered by the computer.

● **Consider multifunction machines:** a combination printer, fax and scanner, for example, can save energy.

● **When costing printers,** make sure you factor in the lifespan and price of cartridge refills.

● **Instead of buying a fax machine,** investigate whether you can use fax software and your modem; or, if you have a scanner, scan documents and send them as emails.

● **If you need a fax machine,** choose one that uses plain paper, so you can use both sides of each page, and look for models that scan both sides of a page, to save energy.

● **Do you need a photocopier?** If you rarely need copies, use your scanner or fax machine, or a local print shop.

Efficient computing

● **Use your equipment's energy-saving features** and make sure you use sleep mode or switch off your PC when you're not using it.

• **Select the shortest acceptable period of inactivity** before your computer switches to sleep mode.

• **Switch off appliances at the wall** when not using them.

• **If your computer doesn't have energy-saving features,** turn off the monitor when it's not required: the monitor consumes up to 80 per cent of the power used.

Using consumables

• **Choose recycled paper and packaging** and buy folders and binders from recyclable materials.

• **Avoid chlorine-bleached paper:** look for 'chlorine-free' or 'oxygen-bleached' labels.

• **Select the 'draft' or 'rough' print option** to save toner.

E-waste

• **Reuse or recycle peripherals** and other components.

• **Dispose of your old computer responsibly.** Give it to a non-profit organisation or a friend, ask if the manufacturer will recycle it, or find an accredited computer recycler.

• **Recycle or refill printer cartridges** but first check that using refills won't damage the printer.

laptop wonder

A laptop computer can be just as powerful as a desktop model and consumes as much as 90% less energy.

decorating and cleaning

Clean and manage your house the natural way. Armed with a green cleaning kit and a battery of commonsense strategies, you can tackle dirt and stains, care for your furniture and valuables, and decorate your home without using products which contain potentially harmful chemicals. And you'll save yourself money in the process.

Decorating

Whether you call in the professionals or decide on DIY, it pays to think carefully about the products you bring into your home when giving it a new look.

Floor and wall coverings

Your choice of floor and wall coverings will be influenced by your lifestyle, but it is wise to give equal consideration to the effect these products can have on the air quality in your home. By choosing carefully, you can minimise your exposure to harmful chemicals – and be kinder to the environment.

Flooring and floor coverings

The production of some types of floor covering, such as synthetic carpets, has a high environmental cost, so consider other more natural choices first.

● **Think about your needs in different rooms.** Ask yourself if you really need wall-to-wall carpet. Hard-wearing surfaces are ideal for areas of heavy traffic such as halls and kitchens, whereas softer coverings might be preferable in bedrooms and some living areas.

● **Although attractive and comfortable,** new carpet is likely to emit toxic chemicals due to treatments during production. If you do want carpet, choose one that is made with natural fibres and ideally one without any chemical protective treatments.

● **If carpet underlay is required,** select recycled rubber or natural latex instead of synthetics, which require large amounts of energy to produce and emit harmful gases.

● **Ask your carpet layer to fix the carpet in place** using mechanical fixings – tacks or staples – rather than synthetic adhesives. If adhesive is essential, use a non-toxic adhesive or a water-based adhesive, which has low levels of toxic volatile organic compounds (VOCs).

● **Whatever type of carpet you lay,** ventilate the area well when fitting and do not use the room for at least three days. Avoid laying new carpet in rooms where babies or pregnant women will sleep.

● **Consider timber floors.** Beautiful, hard-wearing and warm underfoot, they are easy to keep clean and don't harbour dust mites. Choose floorboards made from timber harvested from sustainably managed forests or, better still, see if you can source some good-quality second-hand boards. Often the timber in these is far superior to what is currently available. Make sure that new wood has not been treated with chemical treatments or sealants.

Pros &cons

Carpets
Conventional wall-to-wall carpets create a feeling of warmth and luxury. They provide thermal and acoustic insulation and are hard-wearing as well as attractive. But environmental problems arise at almost every stage of their production and use. Their manufacture involves dozens of polluting chemicals. Once in place, carpets give off noxious chemicals, including harmful VOCs, for long periods. Even some natural-fibre carpets are treated with toxic stain repellents and fire retardants that can continue to evaporate for years. Carpets also harbour dust mites that trigger allergies and asthma attacks, and the dust tends to absorb other toxins from the atmosphere.

Natural paints, flooring, furniture and fabrics combine to create a stylish, healthy and eco-friendly environment with abundant natural daylight.

- **Consider stone or slate flooring,** especially if found locally or from a second-hand supplier. Although they are non-renewable, these materials are abundant, durable and absorb heat.

- **For high-traffic areas,** consider using ceramic or terracotta tiles. Durable and easy to clean, they are derived from non-renewable but abundant sources, require relatively little energy to manufacture, do not give off noxious gases and are recyclable.

- **Rather than covering a concrete floor,** try applying a finish to it. Polished concrete is hard-wearing, waterproof and attractive, especially if a natural tint is added when the concrete is poured, and chemical sealants are not necessary.

- **Try to avoid using PVC (or vinyl) flooring.** The manufacture of this flooring releases large amounts of toxic chemicals, it causes as many problems for allergy sufferers as carpet, and on disposal it leaches chemicals into landfills.

CARING FOR FLOORBOARDS

- For unsealed timber, sweep then polish with a cloth impregnated with linseed oil.

- For sealed timber, sweep then sponge-mop with plain water or water and a little detergent.

- Wash an oil-finished timber or polyurethane floor with 1 part methylated spirits to 10 parts hot water. Then buff with a dry cloth.

- Sprinkle sticky patches on an oil-finished floor with flour and then wipe over with a damp cloth.

NATURAL FLOORING

A wide range of natural, renewable flooring materials is available. Make sure the materials have not been treated with chemicals and avoid synthetic adhesives.

BAMBOO (top) Floorboards made from this prolific type of grass are strong, durable and moisture-resistant. They don't warp and are free of knots and other flaws found in wood. Check that no formaldehyde glues or synthetic sealants have been applied.

COIR Derived from the outer husk of the coconut, coir is woven into a coarse material that is very hard-wearing. It's ideal for heavy traffic areas such as halls and living spaces.

CORK (centre) Cork is renewable and recyclable. The bark of the cork tree is harvested once every nine years, then regenerates. Cultivation requires no irrigation, fertilisers or pesticides. Cork flooring is soft, warm and resilient, a good heat and sound insulator and does not collect dust.

JUTE The woven yarn made from fibres of the stalks of the Cochorus or jute plant provides a soft, absorbent material that is ideal for bedrooms but less appropriate for kitchens, bathrooms, stairs or living areas.

LINO (bottom) Made from flax fibre and oil, ground cork, wood, flour and natural resins, then fixed to a natural backing such as jute, lino emits no toxic gases and is antistatic, easy to clean and biodegradable.

SEAGRASS Woven from the fibres of various species of seagrass, this material is tough, hard-wearing and naturally antistatic and stain-resistant. Not suited to damp rooms, nor to high-traffic areas, as its waxy fibres can be slippery.

SISAL The tightly woven yarn made from the fibres of the agave plant produces durable flooring that is naturally antibacterial and antistatic – but it marks and stains easily.

Cleaning carpets

● **Scoop or scrape away all solid spills** with a blunt knife or spoon. Blot liquids with a clean cloth, pressing firmly to soak up all the spill. Proceed cautiously if you are at all concerned about colour-fastness.

● **Try using soda water to get rid of the rancid smells** that can be left behind on carpets from some foods, animal messes and vomit. Or rub a little bicarbonate of soda on the spot with a damp cloth.

● **Pour soda water or mineral water on to liquid spills** on carpets. The bubbles cause the spillage to rise to the surface where you can blot it with a clean cloth.

..... corking flooring!.........
        Because cork comes in tile
form, any damaged or worn areas can be easily
and cheaply replaced.

- **Sprinkle bicarbonate of soda** on natural and synthetic floor coverings to remove grease, dirt and odours. Leave for 15 to 30 minutes and then vacuum up powder. For heavy grease stains you may need to use cornflour.

- **To remove candle wax from carpet** scrape off wax with a blunt knife. Cover with blotting paper, a tissue or brown wrapping paper. Holding a hot iron just above it, blot the carpet with the paper. Use several sheets if needed.

- **Never use an alkaline product** (some laundry detergents are alkaline) on a wool carpet as it can damage the fibres and cause fading of fabric dyes.

Wall coverings

- **Keep things simple.** Do without wall linings and coverings unless they improve efficiency – for example, by acting as an insulator. Choose easy-to-apply finishes such as renders, washes and paints.

- **Think twice about wallpaper.** It might look good and help to disguise an uneven wall, but some wallpapers contain harmful inks and dyes, fungicides and VOCs.

- **Consider cork tiles** for areas where you require good sound and heat insulation. Seal with beeswax or natural oil.

- **For bathrooms and kitchens,** ceramic tiles are easy to clean and discourage the growth of mould and bacteria. Reinforced glass is an alternative for kitchens.

GREENER WALLPAPERING

If your heart is set on wallpaper, investigate eco-friendly options, such as recycled papers printed with water-based inks, and use water-based paste instead of chemical-based glues. To prevent fungal growth, add borax to the paste.

Whether you go for vintage or modern, a tiled bathroom is easy to clean and discourages the growth of mould and bacteria.

Paints, stains and sealants

Under recent EU rules, petrochemical-based paints and sealants will contain progressively lower levels of VOCs. And while a UK-wide voluntary VOC labelling scheme initiated by B&Q makes it easier to compare paint products, an ever-widening range of natural, completely safe alternatives is now available.

- **Try to use paints that are VOC-free** or low-VOC, especially indoors. If you are committed to an all-natural approach, choose lime washes or organic paints made from all-natural ingredients. Look out for the Ecolabel flower, awarded to products that meet strict criteria limiting their impact on the environment, from manufacture to disposal.

- **Think carefully before you choose conventional paint.** Its production involves the use of a cocktail of chemicals and the finished products often contain toxins such as heavy metals and VOCs. After application, these paints continue to emit harmful fumes for several months. Non-biodegradable, they leach chemicals into the ground.

- **Bear in mind that although water-based (acrylic) paints** are generally safer than oil-based paints, they can still contain harmful chemical additives.

- **If you can achieve a smooth surface with minimal preparation,** paint over old paint rather than remove it. Wear a dust mask when sanding to avoid inhaling dust from old paints or varnishes.

- **To remove old paint,** use a water-based, solvent-free paint stripper, a hot-air gun or a scraper and plenty of elbow grease. Avoid using chemical paint strippers as they contain substances such as methylene chloride and dichloromethane, both thought to be carcinogenic.

- **Be wary of old paints containing lead,** used as a drying agent in paint prior to 1950 and now known to be highly toxic. If you are unsure of what you are dealing with, get a paint fragment tested by an expert. If the paint is in good condition, it is often best to leave it in place; otherwise ask a specialist to remove it.

- **To wash down a wall for painting,** use a solution of washing soda and water. Add ½ cup washing soda to 500ml water for a regular solution. For a mild solution, add just 1 tablespoon washing soda to every 500ml water; for a stronger solution, add 1 cup washing soda to every 500ml water.

- **Use a special painter's mask when painting.** These are available from hardware and DIY stores and are different from dust masks, which should not be used as they will trap fumes near your mouth and nose.

- **Whatever type of paint you are using,** always make sure that the room you are decorating is well ventilated. If possible, air the room for a week before using it after painting (especially if it's a bedroom).

Levels of VOCs in a newly painted house can be up to 1,000 times higher than outdoor levels

SAFER PAINTS

Some alternatives to conventional paints are listed below, with the safest options first.

- **MILK PAINT**
A mixture of casein, a protein found in milk, and earth pigments, milk paint has a smooth matt finish suitable for interior walls and furnishings.

- **LIME WASH** Made from lime and natural pigments, lime wash gives walls – exterior and interior – a soft, weathered look.

- **NATURAL/ORGANIC PAINTS** are usually made from vegetable and mineral extracts bound with natural oils or resins. Some natural paints still contain conventional pigments such as titanium oxide and natural solvents that can be low-level irritants.

- **VOC-FREE PAINTS** These have the same make-up as conventional paints, but exclude the harmful VOCs. They tend to be expensive.

- **LOW-VOC PAINTS** These are made from petrochemicals but with reduced levels of VOCs. They may still contain harmful chemical additives. Check the labels on the can for the VOC content.

Using natural paints

- **Try to use natural paints soon after purchase,** as they contain few preservatives and so don't last long.

- **Allow for extended drying times.** Natural paints don't contain chemical drying agents.

- **Some natural paints are thinner than regular paints.** When painting a ceiling, cut a slit in a sponge and thread it onto your brush to prevent paint running down your arm.

- **Wear a mask when you are mixing powders** as some can be caustic.

- **Remember: natural paint leftovers can be added** to your compost! Even so, try not to buy more than you need.

Sealing wood

- **Avoid polyurethane wood sealants.** Many contain di-isocyanate, a respiratory irritant, and all contain a range of other VOCs. The most toxic are the two-part coatings that have to be mixed before application. Oil-modified urethanes generally release less gas than moisture-cured ones.

- **Use beeswax to create a durable, attractive surface.** The wax can be applied on top of natural oil.

- **Consider natural stains.** Lime finishes come in a range of colours that give an aged look to wood while highlighting its grain. Other washes and stains give timber a light colouring while allowing the grain to show through.

- **Remember that some natural sealants,** such as oils and beeswax, may need to be applied more often than synthetics to keep the wood in good condition.

- **Try shellac for painting wooden shelves** and to seal treated wood or wood-composite products that may emit toxic fumes. Shellac is 100 per cent natural, easy to apply, smells good and dries to a matt finish in 2–3 hours. It can be used on plain wood surfaces or painted ones.

CLEANING UP

- To clean water-based paints off brushes, wipe off the excess with newspaper, then wash the brushes in a bucket of water. Pour the water on waste ground, away from drains.

- To clean brushes used with solvent-based (oil-based) paints, use a non-toxic thinner or natural turpentine-based cleaner; or boil the brushes in vinegar then wash in water. Some mineral turpentines contain benzene, a carcinogen.

- Never pour unused paints or solvents down the drain. Allow residual paint in cans to dry out naturally or soak up with newspaper. Or donate larger quantities of paint to a paint reuse scheme (see page 124).

Renovating

There's often no need to buy replacements for worn but otherwise useful items. You can breathe new life into your old furniture at little or no expense.

Furniture restoring

With some basic precautions and a little care, good furniture can last for many years. Regular maintenance with gentle cleaners and conditioners such as beeswax, vinegar and pure soap can bring new life to well-used furniture and preserve its natural sheen.

Caring for wooden furniture

● **Keep wooden furniture out of sunlight** and it will last longer (this also applies for upholstered pieces). Ultraviolet rays bleach and damage both wood and fabric.

● **Avoid placing good furniture in very damp or very dry places,** or near hot fires, heating vents or radiators. With high moisture levels wood expands, but as the atmosphere becomes less humid, wood may develop cracks. Cracking may also occur in very dry or hot conditions, or if the furniture is subjected to extreme temperature variations.

● **Start any cleaning routine with dusting,** preferably using a slightly damp cloth. If you apply polish to dusty wood, you'll grind in the dirt and may damage the surface.

● **Clean wood, if necessary, with a mild soap and water.** For unfinished wood or finishes other than polyurethane, use the suds only on a barely damp sponge or cloth. This avoids overwetting.

● **To clean and condition unfinished and lightly finished surfaces,** try a simple polish made from equal amounts of olive (or linseed) oil and white vinegar mixed with a few drops of essential oil. Apply it with a soft cloth.

● **To clean raw pine,** always use cold water and soap, as hot water may turn it yellow. To remove grease spots, rub with fine-grade sandpaper and wipe with a damp cloth.

● **A French-polish finish** is susceptible to damage by heat and all solvents, including water. Wipe the surface

FURNITURE POLISH

Commercial polishes and waxes may contain ingredients such as phenol, nitrobenzene or petroleum distillates. These substances are highly flammable and are also harmful when inhaled or ingested or if they come into contact with the skin. Normally remaining in the environment for only a few days, they may persist for longer when released in larger amounts or over an extended period. Some polishes also contain fine abrasive materials, which may wear away a finish over time.

..... musty magic! ....
To banish musty smells, sprinkle upholstery with bicarbonate of soda, then vacuum up after an hour or two.

make it yourself

Furniture polish

125g beeswax, grated
500ml raw linseed oil (for dark wood)
or olive oil (for pale wood)
1 tsp lavender or rosemary essential oil

Melt the wax in a heatproof bowl over a saucepan of simmering water. Carefully add the oil and stir over heat for 3 minutes. Remove from the heat and stir in the essential oil. Transfer to a clean jar and allow to set.

Using a soft cloth, rub polish sparingly into the wood, leave for 30 minutes, and then polish off.

NATURAL CARE TIPS FOR WOODEN FURNITURE

WOOD POLISH
Use a little milk on a soft cloth to polish highly grained wood, such as walnut and cherry, and it will give the wood a good sheen.

ERASE INK BLOTS
Salt and lemon juice rubbed over the stain often works for bleaching ink stains out of bare wood. On a finished surface, ink blots are best ignored, especially if the piece of furniture is an old desk or bureau.

carefully with a barely damp cloth. If it needs waxing, use only pure, softened beeswax, always working in the direction of the grain.

● **To keep dust from settling quickly on wooden furniture,** mix 1 litre of water with 1 teaspoon of vinegar and 1 teaspoon of glycerine in a container. Pour a little of the mixture on to a soft cloth and wipe it over your furniture.

● **To brighten a dulled lacquer or varnish finish,** mix a little traditional white, non-gel toothpaste with water and rub it on with a cloth.

● **To fix blistered veneer,** cut with a trimming knife, slide wood glue underneath with a palette knife and press the veneer back into place. Cover with greaseproof paper and put a heavy weight on top.

● **You can remove old French polish** (shellac) with methylated spirits and elbow grease.

Quick fixes for stains and scratches on wood

● **Treat scratches on light wood with petroleum jelly** or 1 teaspoon each of vinegar and raw linseed oil mixed together. For darker wood use equal quantities of red wine and raw linseed oil.

● **Scratches on light wood can be covered up** with white or beige shoe polish. On darker wood use brown shoe polish; on ebony you can use black shoe polish.

● **Rub half of a kernel of walnut over scratches** on walnut furniture to help fill them in.

● **Get rid of water marks on wood** by rubbing them with toothpaste. For stubborn stains, add some bicarbonate of soda, then polish with a soft cloth.

● **Remove spilt wax** by placing a piece of kitchen towel over it and pressing lightly with a warm iron. The wax should melt and be absorbed by the paper. Repeat the process if necessary. Wipe over the area with a weak solution of water and vinegar and dry with a clean cloth.

CHECKLIST

✓ Wax protects and nourishes unfinished or lightly finished wood as well as fills in fine scratches and gives wood a soft sheen.

✓ Always dust and clean before waxing, otherwise you'll seal in the dirt.

✓ Choose a solid wax based on beeswax (or make your own).

✓ Allow the wax to dry before giving the surface a good buff with a soft cloth.

✗ Avoid using cream waxes, which contain solvents that may soften and remove lower layers of wax.

Reviving upholstery

- **Revive faded colours** by rubbing the fabric gently with a weak water and white vinegar solution (4:1).

- **To remove fluff from upholstery,** soak a chamois leather in white vinegar and rub it gently over the surface of the fabric.

- **Fresh stains can sometimes be removed** if you sprinkle them with cornflour or salt. Leave for 15 minutes or so to absorb the stain then wash off.

- **Stubborn stains disappear** when rubbed with shaving cream. Allow the cream to soak in for a while, then rub down with a cloth and clean water.

- **Use a little glycerine soap** on a damp cloth to give leather furniture a gentle clean. Rinse off.

- **Polish and nourish leather furniture** by rubbing the furniture gently with a mixture of 1 part vinegar to 2 parts linseed oil. Buff to a gentle shine using a soft, clean cloth.

To keep your upholstery dust-free, vacuum it regularly. Dusty furniture eventually becomes dirty.

To remove **tea, coffee and red wine stains,** sponge the fabric with a solution of **4 tablespoons borax dissolved in 600ml water** and blot with a paper towel pad

METAL MAKEOVERS

- Reuse aluminium foil, crumpled into a wad, to rub away pinprick rust spots on chrome furniture and taps.

- Rub pitted chrome with fine steel wool and methylated spirits to remove rust spots. Polish with a little olive oil.

- Polish painted iron or aluminium furniture with beeswax for extra protection, especially if it is to be used outside.

- Use scrapers, wire brushes and sandpaper to remove rust from cast iron before priming and repainting.

- To loosen water-based paint, soak the item in boiling water. For oil-based paint, soak overnight in a bucket of water with 250g fireplace ash, if you have it.

Cleaning

By rethinking your approach to cleaning your home, you can save money, create a healthier living space and reduce your impact on the environment.

Keeping a clean home

A clean home is both a pleasure to live in and essential for healthy living. Maintaining a regular cleaning routine keeps dirt under control, and moulds and allergy-producing substances in check. Cleaning little but often is the key – if you catch dust and spills before they turn to grime, you won't need harsh chemical cleaners.

Ten steps to better cleaning

1 **Stop the dirt before it comes inside.** Place good-quality dirt-absorbing mats at all entrances to the home. Your carpets will stay cleaner and last longer.

2 **Initiate a shoe-free policy in the household** to avoid the problem of tracking in oil and dirt from outside. Provide a shoe rack at the door and a chair nearby, to encourage people to oblige.

3 **Try to tidy up as you go.** If you haven't the time, clear up small messes as they occur and you won't have a big job to deal with at the end of the day.

4 **Instead of reaching for the strongest chemical** cleaner first, look for environmentally responsible cleaning alternatives. They will usually work just as well.

5 **Act fast on spills and stains.** Not only will you find that your cleaning is more effective, you'll also need fewer chemicals to do the job.

6 **Give cleaners time to work** and you'll find you need less of them. Leave mould and oven cleaners to work overnight, for example.

7 **See how little you can get away with.** Use less when applying household cleaners, whether they are commercial brands or more natural alternatives. You may find that a wipe with a damp cloth is all that's required.

8 **Use elbow grease.** Brushes, scourers and cloths are the first line of defence against dirt and reduce the need for harsh, fast-acting chemicals.

9 **Use recycled materials** to clean kitchen and bathroom surfaces. Old cotton T-shirts and towels are perfect. They're economical and longer-lasting than disposable wipes and paper towels.

10 **Work out a minimum cleaning routine** to keep your home functioning efficiently. That way, even if you're extra busy, at least you know you've covered the basics each week.

Microfibre know-how

● **Start with an all-purpose cloth or mitt.** There are various grades for different applications, from cleaning glass to washing cars.

● **Buy wisely** – the most expensive microfibre cloth is not necessarily the best, but the very cheapest tend to be inferior and don't last as long.

● **Clean your windows with a microfibre cloth** just after it's come out of the washing machine. It will be at just the right dampness after the spin cycle.

● **Damp microfibre cloths will remove bacteria.** Wipe the surface dry after use as an extra precaution.

Vacuum cleaners

A weekly vacuum will pick up dust before it turns to grime and keep dust mites at bay. Consider these points when buying your next cleaner.

● **Higher wattage vacuum cleaners** don't necessarily have a more powerful suction. Do your homework before buying, ask for a demonstration and make sure the machine you choose suits the surfaces you want to clean.

● **Do you want a bag or non-bag system?** Disposable paper bags make less mess than canisters or fabric bags, but are less cost-effective.

● **Ask about the filter system used in the vacuum cleaner,** especially if anyone in your family is asthmatic or suffers from allergies. The best filters, known as HEPA (high efficiency particulate air) filters, capture minute particles of dust and allergens that would otherwise be blown back into the air through the vacuum's exhaust system.

● **Consider models with an indicator** that alerts you to when the bag or canister needs emptying or replacing. Full bags waste energy – both yours and the motor's.

Pros & cons

MICROFIBRE CLOTHS
Although made of synthetic fibres (polyester and polyamide), microfibre cloths do have a place in the eco-friendly tool kit. Because of the way the fibres are arranged, microfibre cloths pick up dirt without the addition of chemical cleansers. They're much more absorbent than natural textiles, pick up and hold dirt and grease without scratching, are easy to use on almost any surface and can be washed and used repeatedly. Buy good-quality cloths that will last and make worthwhile the energy used in their production.

......be fibre-friendly......
When laundering microfibre cloths, avoid fabric conditioners. They coat the fibres and render the cloths useless.

● **Look for models with a variable power button,** which allows you to use less suction on delicate items.

● **A floor turbo attachment will use more energy,** but will increase carpet cleaning efficiency.

● **If you clean mostly carpet,** look for a cleaner that offers pile adjustment. This saves wear and tear on your carpet and the vacuum motor.

Cleaning tool kit

You need surprisingly few tools to clean your home. Recycle from everyday staples when possible and when buying choose good-quality equipment that will last.

Recycle **T-shirts and cotton towels** Cut to usable sizes for a constant supply of absorbent cleaning cloths. **Single cotton or wool socks** Pull on to your hand and use as a duster. **Toothbrushes** Use to clean around taps and hard-to-access areas. **Shaving brushes** and **unwanted paintbrushes** Use for dusting delicate items. **Spray bottles** Keep on hand for homemade cleaning solutions.

Buy new **Long-handled soft broom** More expensive brooms with good-quality bristles will pick up the dirt better and will last longer. **Dustpan and brush** Buy several and store them near high-activity areas ready for quick clean-ups. **Long-handled sponge mop and bucket** Choose good-quality mops with sturdy replaceable heads. For the kitchen **Washing-up brush**, **vegetable scrubbing brush** and **fine steel wool scourer**. For the bathroom **Toilet brush** and **bucket**.

Using cleaning aids such as **scrubbing brushes and steel wool** reduces the need for fast-acting chemicals

Choose carefully

Knowing which chemicals to avoid in commercial cleaning products is difficult. It's a complex subject and not everyone agrees on which substances are harmful. Many labels are short on ingredients and, even when they are included, they are not easy to understand. Before selecting a chemical cleaner try to find out what the ingredients are likely to be.

Cleaning agents: what's in them?

If you want to know what's in a cleaner or detergent you use regularly, and the ingredients are not on the label, you will need to contact the manufacturer.

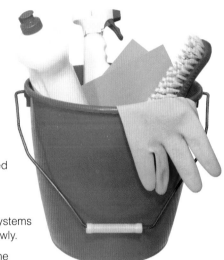

● **Use the caller information number** on the product label (usually a free-phone number) to enquire about ingredients or ask for a safety data sheet, which will identify any dangerous ingredients. Most companies will oblige – if not, it may be wise to select an alternative product.

● **Some personal care and cleaning products contain a class of surfactants** (dirt removers) called alkylphenol ethoxylates, despite an EU ban on their domestic use in 2002. Two of these (nonylphenol and octylphenol) are hormone disrupters, which mimic the hormone oestrogen and can affect the reproductive systems of fish, birds and mammals. They also biodegrade slowly.

● **The antibacterial agent triclosan** is found in some dishwashing liquids, antimicrobial soaps and dishcloths. It has been found to react with chlorine in water to form chloroform, which is closely related to dioxin and is not readily biodegradable.

● **Volatile organic compounds** (VOCs), including toluene and trichlorethylene, are found in some spot removers and floor waxes and polishes. Some VOCs are linked to cancer, and others, such as formaldehyde (formalin), an ingredient in some laundry detergents, can cause health problems such as nausea, wheezing and skin rashes.

● **Quaternary ammonium compounds,** such as benzalkonium chloride, cetrimonium bromide, quaternium-15 and quaternium 1-29, are used in many cleaning products. They can cause irritation to the eyes and have been linked with a variety of allergic symptoms in susceptible people.

USE IN MODERATION

● Hydrogen peroxide is an oxidising bleach that breaks down quickly into water and oxygen. Use in preference to bleaches that contain chlorine.

● Methylated spirits should be 95 per cent alcohol (ethanol, usually derived from plants) and 5 per cent methanol (a petroleum by-product that is poisonous). Do not inhale or ingest and do not tip down the drain.

● Ammonia is generally not considered harmful to the environment. However, it can be harmful to people with respiratory problems. Use in a well-ventilated area and never mix with chlorine bleaches.

SAFETY FIRST

If you choose to use chemical cleaners, take care to minimise risks to your health.

- Open windows so that fresh air can dissipate fumes and pollutants.

- Wear rubber gloves and long-sleeved clothing. For heavy-duty jobs, always wear a mask and goggles.

- Do not mix cleaners. You risk creating a more toxic substance.

- Use rub-on cleaners rather than sprays to avoid inhaling.

- Rinse cleaned surfaces well to remove chemical residues.

- Avoid using chemical cleaners in cooking and eating areas.

Air fresheners

- **Don't use a manufactured smell** to cover up another smell. Air fresheners can contain health-hazardous VOCs.

- **Some air fresheners contain paradichlorobenzene,** a chlorine derivative linked to liver and nerve damage.

- **Be careful when buying essential oils.** Some have been diluted with synthetic scents, which can be harmful to inhale, particularly for people with allergies. Look for labels that state '100 per cent pure essential oil', or similar.

Household bleaches

- **Watch out for chlorine,** which is present in many household bleaches and mould removers. It can react with other dangerous organic matter in sewage to form toxic, very persistent chemicals called organochlorines.

- **Avoid chlorine in the form of sodium hypochlorite,** a lung and eye irritant that releases toxic fumes when mixed with ammonia or acid-based cleaners (including vinegar).

Laundry products

- **Look for 'no phosphate' on the label.** This means no added phosphate and a background level of less than 0.5 per cent.

- **Some cleaners and detergents** are perfumed with artificial musks. They're persistent chemicals, both in the human body and the environment; some may be neurotoxic.

Oven cleaners

- **Avoid cleaners with sodium hydroxide** (caustic soda). This is highly corrosive and can cause severe irritation, deep burns and blindness.

- **Products labelled 'non-corrosive'** may contain the solvent ethanolamine, that can cause headaches and asthmatic reactions, and affect the central nervous system.

- **Diethyl glycol alkyl ethers** are found in some oven cleaners and have been linked with birth defects.

Toilet cleaners

- **Many commercial toilet cleaners** contain corrosive acids and dyes and deodorisers that irritate eyes and skin and may be carcinogenic. Some use paradichlorobenzine, a chemical solvent linked to liver and nerve damage.

....don't risk it!.....

Never use strong chemical cleaners near children. Even small quantities can affect them adversely.

Greener cleaners

Cleaning without chemicals is not only possible, most of the time it's equally effective – and far less expensive. Natural cleaning products are also much safer for us and for the environment.

The greener cleaning kit

● **BICARBONATE OF SODA** Use bicarb (baking soda) when you need a mild abrasive. It's composed of sodium bicarbonate, a slightly alkaline substance, which has very low toxicity, and cleans by forming a mild detergent when it reacts with grease and oil.

● **BORAX** A naturally occurring alkaline mineral salt, borax will dissolve grease, remove stains, deodorise, disinfect, bleach, inhibit mould, soften water and fabric – and kill ants. It doesn't persist for long in the environment, but it is toxic if ingested, so use with care, especially around pets and small children. It can usually be bought or ordered from chemists.

● **GLYCERINE** A by-product of the soap-making process, glycerine is a useful cleaning ingredient because it helps mix oil with water and dissolves many forms of dirt. Most glycerine comes from vegetable oil or animal fats (tallow), but about 10 per cent is produced from petroleum.

● **LEMON JUICE** Squeeze a lemon for a milder and much better smelling substitute for bleach. It's also good for inhibiting mould growth, deodorising and removing stains.

● **SALT** This is excellent for scouring pans and kitchen utensils as the grains act as a mild abrasive as well as a disinfectant.

● **SOAP FLAKES** Buy pure soap flakes or make your own by grating a bar of laundry or pure soap. It is 100 per cent bio-degradable and is low in toxicity. Keep soap flakes in an airtight container.

● **TEA-TREE OIL** Use this cleaner and natural disinfectant to finish off after washing surfaces.

● **WASHING SODA** Moderately alkaline, washing soda (sodium carbonate) is a good cleaning staple for the kitchen. It is particularly good for cutting grease, but also removes stains and softens water.

● **VINEGAR** An effective substitute for toilet cleaners. Also use to remove bathroom scum, hard-water (limescale) deposits and tarnishes on metal. Use distilled white vinegar.

BENEFITS OF GREENER CLEANERS

● Natural cleaning products are often cheaper. Less is spent on advertising and the savings are passed on to you, the consumer.

● Homemade cleaning products often contain just one substance – the cleaning agent – and are additive-free.

● People with asthma, allergies or sensitive skins are far less likely to have an adverse reaction to natural cleansers.

● Chemicals that break down fast are better for waterways. Buy cleaners that are low in toxicity and bio-degrade quickly.

Warning
Although washing soda is not harmful to the environment, it is a strong chemical – so you should always wear gloves when using it.

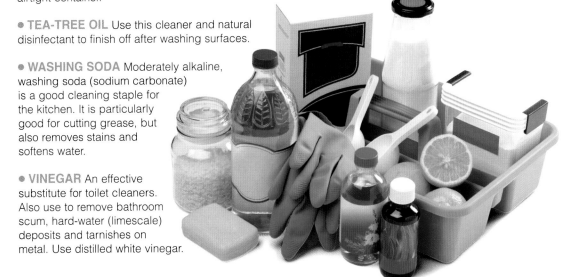

make it yourself

Scouring paste

The simplest cleaner of all. Use for sinks, oven doors, hobs and inside tea-stained mugs.

4 tbsp bicarbonate of soda
1 tbsp water

Mix ingredients into a stiff paste and apply with a damp sponge. Buff residue with a dry cloth.

Bicarb cleaner

A general cleaner, safe for use anywhere in the home.

1 tsp bicarbonate of soda
1 tsp pure soap flakes
squeeze of lemon or dash of vinegar
1 cup warm water

Put ingredients into a spray bottle and shake until soap is dissolved. Spray and wipe with a kitchen sponge.

Vinegar cleaner

All-purpose and long-lasting, this cleaner removes grease and dirt.

Ideal for use on stainless steel sinks, wooden or tiled surfaces and plastic finishes, such as fridge shelves and telephones.

2 cups vinegar
1 cup water

Combine the ingredients in a spray bottle. Shake thoroughly before use, spray on to a soft damp cloth and rub. There's no need to rinse.

Lavender disinfectant

Keeps bathroom surfaces safe and smelling sweet. It also makes a marvellous spray when ironing bed linen.

25 drops lavender essential oil
2 tbsp methylated spirits or vodka
500ml distilled water

Add the oil to the alcohol in a clean dry bottle and leave to dissolve for 24 hours. Add water and decant into a spray bottle. Shake mixture thoroughly before use.

Soap and borax cleaner

This cleaner is so useful you may want to make it up in large quantities. It's great for kitchen surfaces.

2 tsp borax
1 heaped tsp pure soap flakes
3 cups water

Mix ingredients well. Spray and wipe with a damp sponge. Store in an airtight container.

Lemon cream cleanser

This slightly abrasive cleaner is good for baths, basins and hobs.

squirt of phosphate-free liquid detergent
½ cup bicarbonate of soda
1 tsp vegetable glycerine
lemon essential oil

Stir enough detergent into the bicarb to make a soft paste. Add glycerine and several drops of the oil. Apply with a damp sponge, then rinse.

Cleaning 'milk'
This universal cleaning agent is based on a well-tried formula. Gentle on your hands, it is ideal for anyone who has sensitive skin.
- **1 tbsp soft soap**
- **200ml water**
- **1 tsp potash**
- **15g whiting**
- **5 drops lemon essential oil**

Put the soft soap, water and potash into a double saucepan over a low heat, stirring constantly until the soap and potash have dissolved. Whisk in the whiting. Add the lemon oil and pour this cleaning 'milk' into a bottle and seal. It will keep for up to three months.

Pan cleaner
If you have accidentally burnt some food in an aluminium or stainless-steel saucepan, fill the pan with water and leave for an hour before trying this.
- **1 onion**
- **water**
- **1 tbsp salt**

Cut the onion into eight and drop the pieces into the saucepan with sufficient cold water to cover the burnt area. Add the salt and boil for 10 minutes. The burnt residue will dissolve and can be removed with a dishcloth. Boil for longer if the stain remains.

Hob cleaner
This cleaner will make your hob shine. The solution can be made up in larger quantities, as it keeps well for up to four months.
- **250ml water**
- **1 tsp soft soap**
- **½ tsp glycerine**
- **10 tsp vinegar**
- **6 tsp whiting**

Boil the water, then add the soft soap. Mix the glycerine and vinegar in a bowl and pour the boiling water into this mixture. Stir in the whiting then transfer to a bottle and seal tightly.

Rust remover
Removes all rust. To prevent cast-iron cooking utensils from rusting, wipe them with a thin film of cooking oil after washing and drying.
- **1 tbsp citric acid**
- **500ml water**

Mix together the citric acid and water. Brush each spot with the liquid until all the rust has been removed from the surface, then rinse.

Limescale remover
Wipe off surface limescale with vinegar. Stubborn deposits can be shifted with this formula.
- **150ml vinegar**
- **150ml water**
- **¼ teaspoon salt**

Bring the vinegar and water to the boil. Add the salt and dissolve. Apply this liquid to the limescale deposits. Leave for at least an hour. Rinse with clean water and wipe dry.

Kettle descaler
Use this homemade mixture to remove the residue of limescale that appears in kettles and percolators.
- **3 tbsp citric acid**
- **500ml fruit vinegar**

Dissolve the citric acid in the vinegar. Pour this mixture, undiluted, into the kettle or percolator and bring to the boil. Discard the liquid and rinse thoroughly or run clean water through the appliance again.

Window cleaner
Use this vinegar solution for general window-cleaning purposes but if your windows are very dirty use undiluted vinegar or rub them first with half an onion.
- **1 litre water**
- **250ml vinegar**

Pour the water into a bucket, add the vinegar and clean the window panes with a sponge. Dry with kitchen towel and buff with a handful of crumpled newspaper.

Carpet stain foam
Use as a foam for removing stains from carpets and upholstery.
- **2 cups pure soap flakes**
- **½ cup methylated spirits**
- **25ml eucalyptus oil**

Shake all the ingredients together in a large jar until combined. Add a little hot water if the mixture is too hard to mix – but leave it fairly thick. Store in a sealed jar.

To use: stir 2 to 3 tablespoons of mixture into 1 litre of very hot water and whisk until suds form.

Rub just the foam suds over the carpet or upholstery stain and leave for 10 minutes. Wipe away with a damp sponge dipped in white vinegar (this neutralises the alkalinity left by the foam). Blot thoroughly with a clean pad.

For extra tough stains, add ¼ cup washing soda to the hot water with the foam mix and whisk until soda crystals have completely dissolved.

A clean kitchen

The kitchen is the room with the greatest potential for accumulating grease and spills. If you get into the habit of a daily cleaning routine, it's easy to keep it clean without using harsh commercial products. If you add a little time into the equation, it's possible to get rid of even hard-to-remove dirt using gentle cleaners.

Routine cleaning

● **Use a solution of salt** – about a teaspoon to a cup of water – to clean the sink. It's extremely effective and almost cost-free.

● **Keep the drains clear.** Catch food debris with a sink strainer. Washing coffee grounds down the plughole will keep your drainpipes clear.

● **Don't put the fat and oil from saucepans down the drain.** Scrape into an old milk carton, freeze, then throw into the garbage bin. This way the oil won't leak into your bin.

● **Clean fridges once every few weeks.** Check use-by dates on cartons and jars and get rid of perishable foods that are past their prime. Don't use commercial cleaning products on fridge shelves – they may contain harsh solvents that damage the plastic. Instead, wipe them down with a paste of bicarbonate of soda and water.

● **Check the seals on bottles and containers in the larder or storecupboard** every six months or so and wipe up any spills as they tend to attract kitchen pests.

● **To clean and deodorise a microwave oven,** add the juice and skin of a lemon to a bowl of water and place

Bicarbonate of soda is an excellent and economical all-purpose cleaner in the kitchen. **It's gentle enough** to use in fridges and on chrome and aluminium without scratching

inside the microwave. Run on high for 2–5 minutes. Remove and wipe the oven interior clean. Always cover food in the microwave to cut down on spills and splatters.

● **Wipe over shiny stainless steel oven hoods and extractor fans** with a damp cloth sprinkled with a little bicarbonate of soda. Buff with a clean dry cloth.

● **Stainless-steel sinks retain their shine** if wiped with whiting and vinegar. Put some whiting in a bowl and pour on sufficient vinegar to form a paste. Apply the mixture to the sink. Wash off afterwards and polish.

Dealing with baked-on dirt

● **Sprinkle saucepans with washing soda.** Gently add boiling water and leave for 30 minutes before washing as normal. Alternatively, pour a thin layer of cooking oil over burnt pans and heat gently. Allow to cool, drain off the oil and wash as normal.

● **Clean an oven dish by dipping it in very hot water** and quickly turning it upside down on a flat surface. Leave for 15 minutes. The trapped steam will loosen the baked-on food residue making it much easier to clean off.

make it yourself

DIY detergent

Use a teaspoon or two in hot water for washing dishes.

- **1½ cups soap flakes**
- **¾ cup water**
- **1½ cups washing soda**
- **1½ cups white vinegar**
- **lemon essential oil**

Bring soap and water to the boil, reduce heat and stir until smooth. Remove from heat, and stir in soda until blended. Add vinegar and a few drops of lemon oil. Store in a sealed bottle.

..... don't make a splash!.........
Use splatter guards on grill pans and don't overfill saucepans – that way you won't have the spills to clean up.

- **Soak oven shelves overnight** in a solution of 1 cup washing soda per litre of hot water. You may need to use the laundry sink, or turn shelves occasionally for even cleaning. Wear rubber gloves for this task.

- **Heat the oven to 200°C, then turn it off.** Place a small bowl of cloudy ammonia in the centre, and a bowl of boiling water on the bottom. Close the oven door and leave overnight. Wipe out in the morning with warm, soapy water.

- **Place wet cloths on the hob** and leave for at least half an hour, or overnight for stubborn stains. The dirt should wipe off without the need for caustic products.

Tricky spots

- **Cut pieces of thick paper or newspaper** to fit on the tops of high cupboards, where grease from cooking settles and gathers dust. Change the paper twice a year and you won't need to clean.

- **Scrub the mildew from the folds of fridge door seals** with an old toothbrush dipped in white vinegar.

- **Pull out the fridge, microwave and dishwasher** once or twice a year to clean behind them. They provide warm dark places where kitchen pests like to hide and breed.

- **Wipe around the knobs of your hob** with the end of a teaspoon wrapped in a scrap of damp cloth.

- **If the U-bend under your sink is blocked,** pour in 1 cup bicarbonate of soda followed by 1 cup vinegar. Once the fizzing has stopped, follow with a kettle of boiling water, then use a plunger to push the blockage through.

Warning

If you have a catalytic self-cleaning oven, do not use any of the cleaning methods described here unless your user's manual says that it's safe to do so.

Wipe out your oven while it is still warm with a cloth or sponge dipped in bicarbonate of soda. If it needs more of a clean, apply a paste of bicarbonate of soda and white vinegar to all surfaces. Leave for an hour, wipe away the residue and rinse with a damp cloth.

Kitchen floors

LINOLEUM AND VINYL

• **Avoid using ammonia products** and abrasive cleaners on linoleum and vinyl as they will dull the surface. Instead, mop with water and a little detergent and rinse.

• **Strong alkaline products make linoleum crack,** shrink and/or discolour. If you use them, rinse the floor well.

• **Remove scuff marks with a pencil eraser,** or rub with neat dishwashing liquid. Wipe clean with a damp cloth.

• **Blot or scoop spillages promptly** to avoid permanent marks. Otherwise, try removing stains with a fine nylon pad and neat detergent, a pencil eraser or all-purpose cleaner.

• **Linoleum stays cleaner** if given a regular treatment with floor polish. Mix 2 tablespoons of soap flakes with 11 litres of water and scrub the floor with a brush. Pour and stir the polish into 4 litres of water and rinse the lino.

• **Black marks from rubber soles** can be removed from lino with a cloth dipped in methylated spirits.

TILED FLOORS

• **Sweep or vacuum over** sealed ceramic or marble tiles and sponge-mop using a bucket of warm water and 2 cups of white vinegar.

• **Use bicarbonate of soda** to remove marks on glazed tiles. For marks on unglazed tiles, rub gently with fine steel wool, using bicarbonate of soda if more abrasion is needed.

• **Use a borax solution** (½ cup borax dissolved in a bucket of hot water) to clean and disinfect tiled surfaces.

KEEPING PESTS OUT OF THE KITCHEN

• Avoid leaving uncovered food on kitchen worktops.

• Wipe up spills immediately.

• Wipe out the oven and grill pan after you've used them.

• Empty rubbish bins regularly.

• To deter ants, place pots of ant-repellent herbs such as mint, chervil or tansy – or use dried bunches of these herbs – near trouble spots.

• A clean sponge sprinkled with sugar makes a sweet trap for ants. They'll soon make their way to the sponge, which you can then drop into boiling water.

• To keep flies away, stand tomato or basil plants on the kitchen windowsill. Alternatively, a few drops of peppermint oil in a jug of water will do the trick.

.....**vanilla freshness** ....

For a **sweet-smelling fridge,**
wipe over the interior with a little
vanilla essence.

A clean bathroom

Some chemicals are absorbed through the skin, so avoid using bleaches and tough abrasives in the bathroom. If anyone in your family has allergies to chemicals, try cleaning the room with a gentle shampoo. Other mild detergents, such as dishwashing liquid, will also work well on tiles and porcelain, especially in conjunction with a fine scouring pad.

Showers and baths

● **A paste of bicarbonate of soda and water** can be used all around the bathroom, from the basin to the shower. Use it with a cloth or a non-scratching scourer.

● **Never use an abrasive cleaner on baths** because it may scratch the surface. A little dishwashing liquid on a cloth is a good alternative.

● **Remove the blue-green stains in the bath** caused by water with a high copper content by rubbing them with a simple paste. Combine 1 tablespoon each of cream of tartar and bicarbonate of soda and add lemon juice drop by drop until a paste is formed. Rub it into the stain with your fingers or a soft cloth. Leave it for half an hour and rinse well with water. Repeat if necessary.

● **Remove rust stains** by squeezing lemon juice over the spot and gently rubbing the rust away with an old toothbrush using a circular motion. Rinse with water and repeat if necessary.

● **To remove limescale deposits from bath taps** wrap taps in a cloth soaked in vinegar for 30 minutes and rinse. For stubborn limescale build-up, repeat as necessary.

● **Clean soap scum from a glass shower screen** by mixing 2 parts salt with 1 part vinegar. Rub on to the screen with a cloth (or even fine steel wool), then rinse and dry.

● **Scrub shower door runners with white toothpaste** using an old toothbrush. Brush with vinegar to rinse. Alternatively, dip a stiff-bristled paintbrush in vinegar and scrub thoroughly.

● **To disinfect the shower recess,** and to clean mould from grout, mix ¼ cup borax with 2 cups very hot water and ¼ teaspoon tea-tree oil. Shake in a spray bottle until the borax dissolves. Spray on surfaces, leave overnight and rinse.

● **After cleaning the shower,** wipe over the tiles and screen with a few drops of almond oil to help prevent the build-up of soap scum.

● **If your showerhead is clogged with limescale,** unscrew it and soak it overnight in a bowl of vinegar. In the morning, remove the deposits with a brush with moderately stiff bristles. If you are unable to unscrew the showerhead, pour the vinegar into a plastic bag, carefully pull the bag up around the showerhead so that the showerhead is immersed in the vinegar and secure the bag to the showerhead's base with rubber bands.

GETTING RID OF MOULD

Mould thrives in a damp environment. For good bathroom ventilation, open windows and/or use an extractor fan. Dry damp towels outside to minimise moisture.

● To stop mould growth, treat susceptible surfaces with 2 teaspoons borax mixed with 1 cup vinegar. Spray or apply with a cloth, leave for 30 minutes and wipe off.

● Apply a paste of bicarbonate of soda and water to clean the grout between shower or floor tiles. Scrub with an old toothbrush and rinse.

● To inhibit mould growth on a shower curtain, dry it with a towel after each shower.

● To remove shower curtain mould, scrub with bicarbonate of soda. Or rub with a paste of vinegar or lemon juice and borax. Rinse well.

BATHROOM CLEANERS

BORAX Kills bacteria and deodorises. Mix with hot water and vinegar or lemon juice to get rid of stubborn stains in toilet bowls. Can also be used instead of bleach to combat recurring mould.

LEMON JUICE An effective and pleasant-smelling alternative to bleach. Useful as a mould-inhibitor as well as a disinfectant. For stubborn mildew stains on shower curtains, rub with lemon juice, rinse and dry in the sun if possible.

SALT Dissolve in water to use as a mild disinfectant in kitchens and bathrooms. Salt is also good for cleaning any surfaces that require a gentle abrasive. Mixes well with vinegar and water for use as a surface cleaner.

SOAP Washes away bacteria and is an important part of basic sanitation. Pure soap flakes are generally available in supermarkets, or you could make your own by grating a bar of pure soap.

TEA-TREE OIL Strong but pleasant-smelling and economical to use as you need only a few drops. Add to hot water when wiping down surfaces.

Basins

- **A pair of tights** works well for cleaning bathroom porcelain that scratches easily. Use them with a mild abrasive, such as bicarbonate of soda or salt.

- **Running low on bicarbonate of soda?** Cream of tartar is a good substitute for cleaning porcelain.

- **Rub lemon juice around plugholes** to remove grease and limescale deposits. An alternative way to remove limescale is by rubbing hard with a plastic scourer and neat dishwashing liquid.

- **For the orange-brown stains** caused by dripping taps, rub vigorously with a mixture of 1 teaspoon salt to ½ cup white vinegar. This also works for hard-water deposits.

- **Use an old toothbrushe** sprinkled with bicarbonate of soda to clean fiddly crevices around taps and plugs. Another good cleaning agent is toothpaste. Try it on taps to give your chrome added sparkle.

- **To remove oily deposits or limescale** from around taps, try wrapping them in a cloth soaked in white vinegar and leave for about half an hour before rinsing.

- **To prevent the bathroom mirror fogging up** while showering, wipe it over with glycerine or a thin film of shaving cream. Buff with a dry cloth.

- **Clean the bathroom mirror** with a solution of ½ cup vinegar in 2 litres water. Also use it to clean window glass and tiles. Unlike plain water, it doesn't leave a water mark.

Toilets

- **Don't put anything except for human waste** and biodegradable toilet paper down a toilet. Anything else can either block the drain or pollute the environment.

- **Put the toilet lid down** before flushing the cistern if your toilet is in the bathroom. Otherwise you risk getting fine mist particles of toilet water all over the room, including your toothbrush.

- **Don't use a proprietary toilet cleaner.** Many contain strong acids and some use toxic chemicals such as paradichlorobenzene.

- **Clean inside the toilet bowl** by sprinkling dampened surface with borax and spray with vinegar (1 cup borax to ¼ cup vinegar). Leave for 1-2 hours to give the solution time to work, then scrub with a long-handled brush and flush.

- **To remove a stubborn toilet bowl ring,** apply a paste of neat borax and lemon juice. Leave overnight, scrub well and flush.

- **Use any general cleaner,** such as a colourless, scent-free dishwashing liquid or soap solution, to clean the outside of the toilet bowl and the toilet seat.

- **Burn off the smell of toilet odours** with an aromatherapy oil burner, a candle or simply light a match. These odours are not harmful, so an open window is generally enough to clear the air.

- **Clean out the toilet cistern every now and then** if you use grey water as it can become smelly. To empty the cistern, turn off the control valve on the inlet pipe. Then flush the toilet; once the cistern has emptied, it won't refill.

Floors

- **To clean linoleum, vinyl or tiles** see tips on page 61.

An old toothbrush with a little bicarbonate of soda is ideal for cleaning round taps and plugs, while toothpaste can add sparkle to your chrome taps.

......`pine' for a smell......
Add a few drops of tea-tree oil to the toilet bowl for extra disinfectant power and a pleasant smell.

Household laundry

There's more to laundry than just keeping clothes clean. Towels, table linen and bedding also need regular attention. Duvets and pillows require less frequent washing but regular shaking, turning and airing to keep them fresh. Always select appropriate washing methods and cycles and use non-toxic products.

Assessing the wash

● **Consider whether you need to wash a garment** after wearing it only once. Freshen it by hanging it in the open air.

● **Many clothes that are labelled 'dry-clean only'** can in fact be hand-washed with care.

● **Hand-wash silks and woollens,** including furnishings, in lukewarm or cold water.

● **To give you more wearings between cleans,** spot-clean clothes that should only be dry-cleaned.

● **Use pure soap flakes for washing by hand:** they are kind to your hands as well as to fabrics.

● **Always hand-wash special items.** Machine washing, even on a gentle cycle, may be rough on clothes.

Machine washing

● **Sort your washing** (whites/coloureds, lightly/heavily soiled, fabric types) so you can choose the optimum cycle for your load and achieve better results.

● **To reduce wear and tear,** empty pockets, turn denim and corduroy inside out, put tights and items with long ties into a mesh bag, and fasten buttons and zips.

Use the elements to dry your clothes. The sun and wind are free, and a clothes line is cheap, long-lasting and **kinder to fabrics** than a clothes dryer

make it yourself

Washing powder

½ cup washing soda
1 cup finely grated pure
   soap
½ cup salt
½ cup borax
½ cup bicarbonate of
   soda

Put the washing soda crystals in a clean plastic bag and crush them finely with a rolling pin. Mix the crushed washing soda with the rest of the ingredients and store in an airtight box or jar.

Use 1 tbsp for a small load, 1½ for a medium load and 2 for a large load. Dissolve the 'powder' in a small amount of hot water and add to the dispenser.

If using it for hand-washing clothes, be sure to wear rubber gloves.

DRY-CLEANING

Dry-cleaning involves the use of perchloroethylene, a potentially toxic chemical belonging to the organochlorine family. Environmentally persistent, it can cause headaches, dizziness, nausea and, with prolonged exposure, liver and kidney damage as well as cancer. Safer alternatives include liquid carbon dioxide and wet-cleaning methods, but they are relatively new and may be hard to find. Check which method your dry cleaner uses. In the meantime, consider if a particular item of clothing needs to be dry-cleaned, and air dry-cleaned clothes in a well-ventilated place for a day or two, to make sure that any chemicals have dissipated.

• **Treat grime and stains before you wash.** Soak the soiled garments overnight, or use a pre-wash stain remover.

• **Most laundry loads can be done in cold water,** which saves energy and saves you money.

• **Put small or delicate items into an old pillowcase,** or special washing bag, before laundering.

• **Wipe out the drum of the machine** and around the door seal after the final load. If the machine tends to smell musty, run a full cycle with 2 cups of vinegar, but no soap.

Pre-wash stain removal

• **Treating dirt and stains before you wash** makes for better results. (See also page 70.)

• Add ¼ cup borax to 500ml water. Pour the mixture into a spray bottle. Use it on stains before washing, remembering to shake the bottle first.

• **For stubborn stains,** mix together 3 tablespoons mild, colour-free dishwashing liquid, 3 tablespoons vegetable glycerine and 375ml water in a spray bottle. Spray. Leave for 15–30 minutes before washing.

• **Rub collars with a paste** made from 1 tablespoon white vinegar and 1 teaspoon bicarbonate of soda.

• **Soak soiled nappies overnight** in a bucket of hot water with ½ –1 cup borax. Wash as usual, adding 1 cup vinegar during the rinse cycle as a fabric softener.

Drying and ironing

• **Whenever possible, dry clothes in the open air:** a clothes line is kinder to fabrics than a clothes dryer.

• **If you have to use the tumbledryer,** choose the 'cool down' or 'permanent press' cycle: cool air creases clothing less than warm air and so reduces the need for ironing.

FABRIC SOFTENERS

● Commercial fabric softeners make your clothes feel soft and smell fresh, but contain potentially harmful chemicals and synthetic fragrances. Try these natural softeners instead.

● Add 1 cup vinegar to your washing machine during the rinse cycle. If your machine is a front-loader, add 2 tablespoons vinegar to the fabric conditioner dispenser.

● For a fresh fragrance, add a few drops of lavender, lemon, rose or eucalyptus essential oil to the vinegar.

● Bicarbonate of soda is also an excellent fabric softener. Add ¼ cup to the wash with a few drops of essential oil.

● After washing a silk garment in mild soapy water, add a dash of methylated spirits to a basin of water and rinse the silk in this to condition the fabric. Iron while it is still damp.

..... sweaty situation!..............

Rub underarm sweat stains with a vegetable glycerine and cream of tartar paste. Leave 24 hours before washing.

- **In bad weather use a fold-away drying rack indoors,** or a ceiling-mounted airing rack in a utility room or laundry.

- **Most clothes won't need ironing** if you smooth and fold everything as you take it down from the washing line.

- **To avoid ironing woollen clothes** such as tailored suits, hang them in the bathroom when you're having a bath or shower. The creases will drop out in the steam.

Bath, kitchen and table linen

- **Wash all towels and linen** regularly and, if possible, dry them in the sun to keep them fresh and hygienic.

- **Before you use new towels,** soak them in a sink of water with a handful of bicarbonate of soda. Then wash as usual, adding 1 cup white vinegar to the final rinse. This softens the fabric and removes any chemicals used in manufacturing.

- **Machine wash all bath towels frequently.** Damp towelling fabric is a breeding ground for bacteria.

- **Soften scratchy towels** by soaking them overnight in a bucket of warm water with ½ cup Epsom salts. Do not rinse.

- **Soak dirty tea towels overnight** in a solution of 2 tablespoons cream of tartar per litre of boiling water, then wash as usual.

- **To disinfect and remove grease from oven gloves** and other kitchen linen, add 2 tablespoons borax to the washing water.

- **To keep linen tablecloths white** soak overnight in a tub of water with 1 cup cream of tartar, then wash as usual.

- **Restore the colours of cotton fabrics** by soaking the items for a few hours in skimmed milk.

BRIGHTER WHITES

Instead of buying off-the-shelf laundry products with chlorine bleaches, try some of these tips to brighten up your whites.

- Add 1 cup each methylated spirits and cloudy ammonia to the washing water to help dissolve and lift off settled dirt.

- Add a tablespoon of baking soda to your washing powder for an extra white, fresh wash.

- Tennis socks regain their former whiteness if you add some lemon peel in a small linen bag to the wash.

- Add ½ cup borax to the machine wash. Borax is active only at temperatures above 60°C, so it must be used in hot water.

- Use old-fashioned washing blue in the final rinse to whiten your whites. Made from the pigment indigo, washing blue creates an optical illusion that makes white fabric look whiter.

- Washing white bed linen with blue towels has a similar bluing effect.

Keep ironing to a minimum. For softer, fluffier towels, shake before pegging them out, and again when dry. Many clothes don't need ironing if you smooth and fold them when dry.

BLANKET CARE

● Soak a very dirty non-woollen blanket for 20 minutes in warm water, then wash it on a gentle cycle in warm water.

● Gently wash a woollen blanket on a machine wool cycle or (preferably) by hand, using warm water, never hot.

● Gently squeeze out the washed blanket, then roll it in towels to remove excess water. Dry flat or draped over several lines on your clothes line.

● To avoid matting the fibres of the wool (felting), don't rub or wring out the blanket.

● Don't tumble-dry a woollen blanket as it could become damaged.

Bed linen and bedding

● **Sheets, pillowcases and duvet covers** should be washed weekly. Pillows, blankets and duvets need less frequent washing but can be laundered when necessary.

● **Machine wash** sheets, pillowcases, duvet covers and mattress protectors and dry them outdoors if possible.

● **Polyester, foam and feather pillows** are all washable, but make sure they are absolutely dry before using them. Regularly air them between washes.

● **Depending on their size, pillows** can be machine washed on a warm, gentle cycle with reduced spin.

● **You can also wash pillows by hand** in soapy water or with wool wash. Rinse several times and dry flat (outside in the shade, if possible) turning over and shaking frequently.

● **Air duvets outside once a week,** if possible.

● **Most duvets** – whether filled with feathers, polyester, cotton, wool or a combination – can be washed. Check the care label for precise instructions.

● **To wash a duvet,** knead it in warm, soapy water (or use wool wash) in the bath. Rinse in several changes of water.

● **It's best not to wring, spin-dry or line-dry a duvet.** To keep the filling evenly distributed, squeeze out as much water as possible and dry the duvet flat – ideally on the grass, on an old sheet – turning and shaking it frequently.

● **If necessary, fluff up pillows and duvets** in the tumble-dryer for about 10 minutes. For duvets, add 2 or 3 clean tennis balls to the drum to help break up the feathers.

Natural stain removal

Stains are inevitable but there's no need to resort to harsh chemicals to deal with them. The key to successful stain removal is to keep a natural stain removal kit on hand and to act quickly. Sometimes all you'll need is nature's greatest solvent – water.

Ten rules for stain removal

1 Take immediate action. The faster you act, the better your chances of completely removing the stain.

2 Mop up the excess. Try to blot up as much of a spill as possible with a clean rag or paper towel. Lift off solids with a knife blade.

3 Don't let the stain dry out. If you can't deal with it straight away, sponge the stain with cold water, spray it with soda water or cover it with a damp towel.

4 Re-lubricate a dry stain. If a stain has dried, rub it with vegetable glycerine before removing it.

5 Don't use hot water. It 'sets' many stains, making them much more difficult to remove. Always use cold or tepid water when you first tackle a stain.

6 Start with the gentlest approach. Often all you need to remove a stain is soda water or a soapy solution.

7 Work from the outside in. To avoid leaving a ring, work from the outer edge of a stain towards the centre.

8 Don't scrub a stain. Instead, place an absorbent pad beneath the stain and dab it with the remover solution, forcing it through the fibres. Change the pad frequently.

9 Work from the back of the fabric to the front. If possible, place the absorbent pad on the stain itself and apply stain remover from the wrong side of the fabric.

10 More is not necessarily better. If a cleaner is not working, don't increase the strength of the solution. Rinse it away, and try something else.

Quick fixes

When you're away from home and disaster strikes, one or more of the following tips might get you out of trouble.

● Sponge with cold water immediately, if possible.

● Pour on a little soda or sparkling mineral water, then mop up the excess.

● Pour salt on an ink spot, then add skimmed milk. Leave for a few hours, then brush off and wash.

● Cover a fruit or wine stain with salt to absorb some of the liquid.

● Sprinkle a grease stain with flour or cornflour.

● Tip white wine on to a red wine stain, then blot with a cloth or paper towel.

NATURAL STAIN REMOVER KIT

FROM THE SUPERMARKET

● Bicarbonate of soda (baking soda)
● Cream of tartar
● Lemon juice
● Methylated spirits
● Phosphate-free, colourless dishwashing liquid
● Pure soap or soap flakes
● Salt
● Soda water
● Vegetable glycerine
● Washing soda (sodium carbonate)
● White vinegar

FROM THE CHEMIST

● Borax
● Cloudy ammonia
● Epsom salts
● Hydrogen peroxide

STAIN REMOVAL AT A GLANCE

Stain	Treat with	What to do
Ballpoint pen	Lemon juice, methylated spirits	Sponge with a cloth dipped in warm lemon juice or methylated spirits.
Beer	Borax, water	Dab with, or soak in, a solution of 2 tbsp borax per 500ml water.
Berries	Vinegar, lemon juice	Rub with vinegar or juice. Leave for an hour or two, then wash.
Blood (fresh)	Cold water, salt	Soak in cold water. Add a handful of salt if stains prove stubborn.
Blood (old)	Vegetable glycerine, cold water	Rub with glycerine to soften, then proceed as for fresh blood stains.
Chocolate, coffee	Borax, water	Dab with, or soak in, a solution of 2 tbsp borax per 500ml water.
Cosmetics	Cloudy ammonia, water	Dab with a solution of 1 part cloudy ammonia per 3 parts water.
Egg, fruit juice	Borax, cold water (not hot)	Dab with, or soak in, a solution of 2 tbsp borax per 500ml water.
Grass	Water, sugar, toothpaste	Dampen stain with water and sprinkle with sugar. Roll up, leave for 1 hour, then wash. Rub stubborn stains with toothpaste.
Grease, oil	Cornflour, talcum powder	Sprinkle spot with cornflour or talcum powder. Brush it off when grease is absorbed and rinse in cold water. Finally wash at as high a temperature as possible for the type of material.
Mildew, mould	Cream of tartar, lemon juice, hydrogen peroxide	Cover spots with a paste of cream of tartar and lemon juice. Leave until dry, then brush off and wash as usual. Or dab spot with a 3 per cent solution of hydrogen peroxide.
Milk	Water, soap, white vinegar	Rinse immediately in soapy water, then soak in water with a dash of vinegar for 10 minutes. Rinse.
Nail polish	Methylated spirits	Dab quickly with a damp cloth, then sponge with methylated spirits.
Rust	Salt, lemon juice	Mix salt and lemon juice to make a paste. Rub into stain, leave 10–20 minutes, then rinse out.
Scorch mark	Vegetable glycerine, borax	Cover the mark with a mix of vegetable glycerine and borax. Leave to dry, then brush.
Shoe polish	Eucalyptus oil, methylated spirits	Place stain on an absorbent pad and dab with oil or spirits, moving the pad frequently so that the stain is over a clean spot.
Soft drink, tea	Borax, warm water	Dab with, or soak in, a solution of 2 tbsp borax per 500ml water.
Turmeric (curry)	Hydrogen peroxide (3 per cent)	Dab stain with neat hydrogen peroxide.
Vomit	Borax, water, liquid antiseptic (for example, TCP)	Scrape up solids. Dab or soak in a solution of 2 tbsp borax per 500ml water, with a few drops of liquid antiseptic.
Wine, red	Soda water, borax, water	Apply soda water immediately. If stain persists, soak in a solution of 2 tbsp borax per 500ml water.
Wine, white	Soda water	Apply soda water immediately, then launder as usual.

Cleaning metals

Whether for sentimental or financial reasons, it makes sense to look after your valuables, and you can do so without resorting to chemical cleaners. But bear in mind that antique silverware can be irretrievably damaged by cleaning and polishing. If in doubt, ask an expert.

Polishing silver

● **Use white toothpaste mixed with a little olive oil** to polish items that can't be immersed; but don't rub too hard.

● **Use an old shaving or stencil brush** to work the polish into the crevices on finely patterned or filigree silver. Cover the bristles with a soft cloth to polish off.

● **Keep a piece of chalk in your jewellery box** to prevent your metal items from tarnishing so quickly.

● **To keep silver cutlery looking bright for longer** wipe it with petroleum jelly after it has been cleaned.

● **Very dirty pewter can be cleaned with warm beer.** Scrub it with a soft brush. Rinse and dry with a soft cloth.

Buttermilk will clean copper. Wipe it on, leave for 10 minutes and then wipe it off

make it yourself

Silver cleaner
This method relies on a scientific reaction, called galvanic coupling, between the two metals.
  a couple of sheets of aluminium foil
  1 tbsp salt
  1 tbsp bicarbonate of soda
Line the bottom of a non-metal bucket with a couple of sheets of foil. Add the salt and bicarbonate of soda. Fill with boiling water.
  Immerse washable silver articles (sterling or plated) in the solution and allow to soak for an hour or two (the foil will darken). Remove the silver to restore its shine.

All-purpose polish
This inexpensive polish may be used to clean brass, copper, bronze, pewter and stainless steel.
  salt
  plain flour
  white vinegar
Combine equal parts of salt and flour, then add just enough vinegar to make a stiff paste.
  Apply sparingly to metal items, then allow to dry for 1–2 hours.
  Rinse off thoroughly and then polish with a soft cloth.
  Do not use much polish, as this may wear away the details of raised designs.

Brass and copper
Any items coated with a protective lacquer should be washed with soapy water. These methods are for uncoated items.
● A salt and lemon juice paste is a good cleaner for brass and copper. Rub it in, then rinse well.

● For stubborn marks on brass, rub with white toothpaste and a little olive oil. Rinse with warm water and polish dry.

● Wipe brass taps, door handles and curtain rods with wax polish to help prolong their shine.

● Shine copper with a cloth dipped in vinegar and sprinkled with salt.

● Polish bronze from time to time with a cloth dipped in linseed oil, then buff with a soft cloth.

Cleaning glass and china

Commercial glass cleaners are often chemical cocktails, containing a range of potentially harmful ingredients that can be inhaled or come in contact with the skin. It's not worth taking the risk. Common natural substances such as lemon juice and salt come into their own in the cleaning and care of glass and ceramics.

Sparkling glass

• **One of the simplest and least toxic** ways to clean mirror and window glass is to spray it with plain soda water, then polish dry.

• **Vinegar and water will clean most windows.** Add a little detergent, if you're still getting streaks.

• **Wipe a glass tabletop with lemon juice,** then polish it with a soft, lint-free cloth.

• **Remove scratch marks with toothpaste.** Work to and fro with a clean cloth.

• **When washing glassware, add a little lemon juice** or vinegar to the rinse water to add extra sparkle.

• **Hand wash glasses in hot water with pure soap,** holding stem-ware by the bowl, not by the more fragile stem. To avoid streaking, rinse and dry straight away.

• **Clean glass bottles with rice.** Drop a few grains into the bottle, add a little water and shake. Rinse thoroughly.

China and crystal

• **Always hand wash fragile, antique or gilded china and crystal** in warm, soapy water.

• **Delicate items should be wiped with a dishcloth** or soft sponge only (not a brush) to prevent scratching.

• **Wash, or at least rinse, delicate china** as soon as possible after use to prevent damage to the glaze.

• **Rinse crystal in clean, hot water** with ¼ cup vinegar added and air-dry upside down on a rack.

• **To clean a red wine stain from a crystal decanter,** put 2 teaspoons each bicarbonate of soda and cream of tartar into the decanter with 1 cup tepid water and shake well. Empty, then add more warm water with a little cloudy ammonia. Shake, empty and rinse well.

• **To remove any hairline cracks** that appear in the glaze on fine china, soak the item overnight in warm milk, then hand wash.

GLASS CLEANERS

Most commercial window cleaners contain ammonia, alcohol and detergents. Some have butyl cellosolve, a chemical that is readily absorbed through the skin and can cause health problems. It is considerably less toxic, cheaper and just as effective to make your own cleaners.

A mixture of crushed eggshells and lemon juice leaves glass sparkling clean. Shake well then rinse.

Breathe cleaner air

Most of us think of our home as a refuge from environmental problems, yet the air indoors can be up to three times more polluted than outdoors. The causes of indoor air pollution are many and varied, but sensible household management can minimise the effects.

Keeping out fumes

Burning fuels and other materials indoors can release gases such as nitrogen dioxide, an eye and throat irritant, and carbon monoxide, which in low doses can cause headaches and fatigue and in high doses can be fatal.

● **Smoking cigarettes indoors** releases hundreds of toxins into the air, including benzene, a potential carcinogen.

● **Keep heaters and stoves in good condition.** If a gas flame burns yellow it may be emitting harmful gases, including carbon monoxide. Service the appliance at once.

● **Check chimneys and flues regularly** for blockages and leaks.

● **If your garage adjoins your home,** ensure there is an air lock or air-tight door between house and garage. Vehicle exhaust fumes contain carbon monoxide and benzene.

Breathe easier

Many household products – paints, furniture, carpets – emit chemical gases. Take a few simple precautions to minimise your exposure. (See also pages 30–31, 34–35.)

● **Avoid synthetic foams and fabrics.** Many emit VOCs.

● **Use low-toxicity cleaning agents** or try products that work without chemicals, such as microfibre cloths.

● **When buying toiletries, cosmetics and perfumes** choose those free of chemicals and synthetic fragrances.

● **Try not to use perfumes and sprays in the bedroom** or any room where you spend long periods of time.

NATURAL AIR FILTERS

Eliminating sources of pollution and ensuring good ventilation are the best ways to improve indoor air quality, but plants can also be used to filter out toxins. Placing three or more in an average-sized room has been shown to reduce levels of VOCs by 50–70 per cent. Proven performers include peace lilies, rubber plants, kentia palms and spider plants.

NATURAL AIR FRESHENERS

Problem	Solution
Kitchen bins	Clean and deodorise with a solution of 1 tsp lemon juice to 1 litre water.
Outdoor bins	To wash, add a handful of washing soda to 1 litre hot water. Sprinkle with bicarbonate of soda to catch residual odours.
Smelly fridges	Place a small open bowl of bicarbonate of soda on one of the refrigerator shelves and change it regularly.
Smelly toilets	Light a scented candle for a few seconds and it will burn off the offending air-bound molecules. A match will also work.

VOLATILE ORGANIC COMPOUNDS

Used in the production of many household items, volatile organic compounds, or VOCs, continue to evaporate, or 'off-gas', at room temperature for years. Many are toxic and their emissions can cause a range of ailments, from eye irritation to fatigue and dizziness; some, such as benzene and formaldehyde, are potentially carcinogenic. By law, new, lower VOC limits in paints, varnishes and stains will apply from 2010. Many paints already carry VOC content labels with a five-band classification from 'minimal' to 'very high'.

● **Avoid aerosol sprays** as they emit a fine mist that is easily inhaled. Use roll-on, pump spray or pump products.

● **Choose a natural air freshener,** such as tea-tree oil.

● **Choose plant-based paints,** varnishes and sealants. If using chemical products, buy only as much as you need, follow the instructions and store in a well-ventilated place.

Breathe easier

Nature contributes to the mix of pollutants we live with from day to day, in the form of moulds, mildew and fungi, pollen, dust mites, bacteria from pet and pest droppings and saliva and skin particles from pets. All will proliferate in damp conditions and can become airborne. In turn they may trigger asthma, allergies and some serious diseases.

● **If dampness is a problem,** check your damp course if you have one, or add a new one.

● **Use extractor fans** to remove moist air from bathrooms and kitchens and to help remove chemical fumes emitted by heaters, hobs and synthetic furnishings and materials.

● **Keep pets clean** and free of insect infestations.

● **Clean, dust and air your home regularly** to minimise pollen, dust mites, animal hair, skin flakes and droppings. Wipe surfaces with a solution of hot water and vinegar to get rid of dust mites.

● **Air beds, bedding and mattresses regularly** to eliminate dust mites, mould and mildew, and wash bedding from time to time (see page 69).

● **Remove furnishings that might attract dust mites,** and replace carpets with hardwood, cork, linoleum or tiles.

● **Sleep with a window open,** if convenient and safe. You spend long periods in the bedroom breathing out carbon dioxide and water vapour, so let fresh air in when possible.

plant paint

Paints and varnishes are a major source of VOCs. Always seek out plant-based or low-VOC products.

the green consumer

Make greener choices when you shop to safeguard your health and protect the environment. You'll also find out how to cut down on your consumption of plastics and packaging, discover ingenious ways for reusing household items and get the low-down on what you can and can't recycle, including how to dispose of hazardous materials.

Buying power

How you shop and spend can make an important contribution to protecting your health and resources, and to the effect you have on the environment.

The choice is yours

Today's consumers are faced with more choice than ever before and a host of sophisticated sales campaigns. The following tips will help you to buy economically, as well as to reduce waste, safeguard health and protect the environment.

Eight eco-smart ways to shop

1 **Do your research before making any major purchase** and don't allow yourself to be persuaded by overzealous salespeople. Sleep on it, if necessary.

2 **Consider the running costs as well as the initial price** of any item you buy. Many environmentally preferred products, such as low-energy compact fluorescent lamps (CFLs) and energy-efficient washing machines, cost more to buy but will save you money in the long run.

3 **Select products made from renewable resources,** such as timber from well-managed forests, wool and silk.

4 **Choose items that are built to last.** For example, choose a sofa that has a hardwood or steel frame rather than one made of softwood or chipboard, which may warp or break easily. You will probably pay more up front, but a well-made piece will last longer.

5 **Buy reusable products rather than disposable ones.** For example, buy washable cloth towels, handkerchiefs, napkins and cleaning cloths rather than paper, single-use varieties.

6 **Buy local produce that is in season.** It is usually cheaper and fresher and has less impact on the environment. It is also normally sold loose rather than in packaging. Markets and roadside stalls are good sources, but some supermarkets also buy from local producers. Support your local farmers' market if you have one.

7 **Look for all-natural,** fully biodegradable, non-toxic products that break down without leaving harmful residues in the environment. (Most materials will biodegrade eventually, but some leave toxic residues.)

8 **Avoid products that have excessive** and/or non-biodegradable packaging. It is estimated that approximately 10 per cent of every shopping bill goes

Buying seasonal, locally grown fruit and vegetables at a farmers' market reduces food miles and helps the environment.

towards paying for packaging – which you normally promptly throw away. Moreover, significant amounts of energy are used in the manufacture of packaging. Purchasing refillable containers can help to reduce this kind of waste.

Break the plastic habit

Plastics have a highly detrimental effect on the environment, but are so much a part of life today that it would be difficult to do without them. However, you can at least reduce how often you use these materials. Think about the plastics you use each week: include plastic bags used for shopping and storing food, plastic containers in the refrigerator and larder, and plastic wrap used to cover food. Then set yourself a goal to reduce your consumption by, say, half. The following tips will help you.

● **Choose glass, ceramic or stainless steel containers** for storing food.

● **To wrap food, opt for waxed or greaseproof paper** or cellophane (made from plant fibre).

● **Substitute paper bags for plastic bags** as often as you can.

● **Avoid prepacked foods.** Buy in bulk whenever possible, taking along your own reusable containers.

● **Try to cut down your use of foods packed** in plastic-lined cans.

● **Look out for degradable freezer bags and bin liners,** which have a less harmful effect on the environment.

● **Take your own reusable bags when you go shopping.** Canvas or string bags are ideal. Bags made from polypropylene can be purchased cheaply from most major supermarkets. Although they are manufactured using non-renewable fossil fuels, they last much longer than plastic shopping bags and can be reused many times.

● **If you have no option but to use plastic bags at the supermarket,** make sure at least eight items go into each one – assuming they are not too heavy.

● **Aim to reuse plastic bags** at least once or twice, preferably more often.

● **Whenever possible, buy plastics that your local council will recycle.** To identify recyclable plastics, manufacturers stamp an identification code on products.

TRUTH ABOUT PLASTICS

Plastics pose a massive environmental problem. Their manufacture is energy-intensive and highly polluting, and only a few can be recycled – and then only once. Plastics never decay and even if incinerated (a process that produces dioxins), 90 per cent of the material remains as toxic waste. Some plastics are suspected of causing health problems. Soft plastics leach harmful VOCs into the air and into food; and phthalates, potentially carcinogenic chemicals also implicated in birth defects, are used to give plastic its flexibility.

...... greener plastic ....

Seek out biodegradable plastic bags, which will break down safely in landfills, without leaving any chemical residue.

An A-Z of popular items

Before reaching automatically for the product you always buy, look through this A–Z list of commonly purchased household items for information about problem ingredients and healthy alternatives. You may be surprised to learn that green choices are often the most cost-effective.

Air fresheners

● **Whether aerosol or wick-based,** many air fresheners contain toxic chemicals, such as formaldehyde and dichlorobenzene, which are both possibly carcinogenic and also tend to persist in the environment for a long time. Most air fresheners also contain synthetic fragrances, which may cause adverse reactions in some people.

● **As alternatives, try bicarbonate of soda or vinegar.** Both will absorb odours at a fraction of the cost of commercial fresheners. Or, if you like a scent, use products made with herbs or essential oils – the main thing is to avoid synthetic fragrances. Also don't forget that fresh air works wonders, too.

Aluminium foil

● **The production of aluminium** requires large amounts of energy and aluminium never breaks down after disposal.

● **Try to use aluminium foil sheets and containers sparingly,** reusing and recycling whenever possible. Recycling aluminium uses only 5 per cent of the energy used in producing new aluminium.

Baby bottles

● **Clear plastic baby bottles** are usually made of polycarbonate, a plastic that has been shown to leach out minute amounts of the hormone disruptor Bisphenol A, especially when heated.

● **Polycarbonate is one of several plastics** identified by a number 7 inside the recycling triangle symbol. As an alternative, look for glass bottles or safer kinds of plastics, such as polyethylene (recycling symbol 1, 2, 4) or polypropylene (symbol 5). Contact the manufacturer if you are unsure.

Babycare products

● **Baby oil often contains mineral oil,** a petroleum derivative. Gentler, more environmentally friendly choices include cold-pressed vegetable and nut oils such as grapeseed, jojoba, almond and apricot kernel.

● **To protect your baby's skin from the detergents,** preservatives and fragrances found in many commercial soaps, shampoos and creams, choose plant-based alternatives.

Seek out **biodegradable plastic bags** which will break down safely in landfills without leaving any chemical residue

Batteries

● **Consider using rechargeable** nickel metal hydride (NIMH) batteries. These require a charger unit and cost about three times as much as standard alkaline batteries, but can be recharged more than 500 times, making them much more economical in the long run. And with some models, recharging takes only 15 minutes, which is usually quicker than going to the shops! You'll also help to reduce the amount of waste going to landfill.

Bin liners

● **Instead of reaching for standard plastic bin liners,** read the labels and choose biodegradable bags instead. Slightly more expensive plastic bags, made from starches derived from plants such as corn and potato, will biodegrade in about 3 months.

Bottled water

● **Plastic bottles for water** contribute to environmental pollution both in their manufacture and their eventual disposal. It is much more cost-effective and kinder to the environment to drink filtered tap water.

● **Avoid buying mineral water** with a high sodium content – above 30mg sodium per 100ml.

CLEANING PRODUCTS

Household cleaning and laundry products contain a huge array of synthetic chemicals, some of which are harmful to both humans and the environment. (See also Greener cleaners, page 55.)

ALL-PURPOSE CLEANERS Try to buy fewer cleaning products. One simple, green, all-purpose cleaner, whether home-made or a commercial product, is really all you need to do the vast majority of household cleaning jobs.

PHOSPHATE-FREE DETERGENTS Choose unperfumed, phosphate-free or low-phosphate laundry powders and liquids.

BIODEGRADABLE PRODUCTS Try to use only products that are 80–100 per cent biodegradable and free from phosphates, petrochemicals, optical brighteners (or fluorescers), enzymes, chlorine and caustic soda.

PRODUCTS WITH WARNINGS Many products do not carry a full ingredients list, but they are required by law to carry warnings if they are hazardous or poisonous. Avoid products that carry such warnings. If they're toxic enough to poison or burn you, they're best left on the shelf. (The exception is borax: though poisonous if ingested in large amounts, it still has a valuable place in a green cleaning kit.)

ECO-FRIENDLY LABELS Look for labels that indicate that a product is eco-friendly, but read such labels critically – 'natural', 'organic' and 'biodegradable' are often used very loosely and may not mean much. For example, almost everything will break down (biodegrade) eventually: you need to know that it will do so in weeks rather than decades!

PACKAGING Consider how the cleaning products you buy are packaged: do they come in a larger size or in bulk? In a concentrated form? In a recycled container?

Cat litter

● **Two popular types of cat litter** are a clay-based product and a clumping litter. Clay for litter is obtained by potentially environmentallly harmful strip-mining and may contain crystalline silica, a lung irritant. Clumping litters often contain sodium bentonite, which can cause respiratory problems in cats and harm to kittens, who ingest it after licking their fur.

● **Look for 100 per cent biodegradable,** non-clay organic products, such as 100 per cent recycled paper or organic wheat. If odour is a problem, sprinkle the litter with bicarbonate of soda.

Coffee

● **Choose to drink natural ground coffee,** because huge amounts of energy are consumed in the dehydration of instant and decaffeinated varieties.

● **Try to avoid coffee grown using chemical pesticides and fertilisers.** Choose certified organic brands, and look out for the 'fair trade' label.

● **If you like decaffeinated coffee,** choose one that has been decaffeinated using the water extraction or carbon dioxide methods. Some methods involve the use of chemical solvents such as methylene chloride, which has been linked to cancer in humans.

Coffee filter papers

● **Buy reusable unbleached cotton filters** or disposable unbleached or oxygen-bleached paper filters. Chlorine-based bleaching leaves dioxin residues in the filters and releases dioxins into the environment. Dioxins have been identified as carcinogens by the World Health Organisation.

● **Consider buying a reusable gold mesh filter** – or change to plunger or espresso coffee-making methods.

Glue

● **The most dangerous ingredient in many glues** is the solvent – rapid-drying solvent-based glues give off toxic fumes. Select a water-based rather than solvent-based glue.

● **It is difficult to find alternatives** for special-purpose adhesives such as epoxy glues, contact adhesives, rubber cements, instant glues and hobby glues. But most contain toxic ingredients, such as hexane, xylene, trichloroethane, acetone and toluene, so always use in well-ventilated areas.

● **The least toxic glues are white glue** (PVA), and paste-based glue sticks. For children, the safest is a flour-and-water paste.

Light bulbs

● **Try to replace as many incandescent light bulbs and halogen lights** as possible with energy-saving compact fluorescent lamps (CFLs). These cost more initially, but can last 15 times longer and use up to 80 per cent

FABRIC SOFTENERS

Fabric softeners are designed to stay in your clothes for a considerable time and can slowly release a range of chemicals that have been linked with a variety of ailments. But there are safer, natural alternatives.

● Use bicarbonate of soda or vinegar to soften your wash. Add an essential oil if you like fragrance.

● Try re-usable 'drier balls' in your tumble-dryer. Their tips massage the textile fibres, acting as a natural fabric softener. The balls also reduce the drying time by 25 per cent because they help air to circulate around the machine. Buy them by mail order or from hardware stores.

less energy than incandescent and halogen bulbs, which waste most of their energy as heat. Energy-saving bulbs are available in various shapes, sizes and tones.

Make-up

● **It is difficult to find any eye make-up, foundation, lipstick or blusher** that does not contain any chemical products. The vast majority contain preservatives of some kind, because unpreserved cosmetics are prone to bacterial growth.

● **Cosmetics may also contain penetration enhancers** such as PEG and TEA, which sensitise the skin and allow chemicals to enter the body. TEA (triethanolamine) can form carcinogenic compounds.

● **Look for the most natural,** least fragranced options, preferably preserved with vitamins A, C or E. Use the internet to check what products are available.

Nappies

● **Even allowing for their manufacture** and the necessarily high level of washing required, cloth nappies are generally a more eco-friendly choice than disposable nappies. One modern nappy system consists of a fitted non-plastic, waterproof cover with elasticised legs and waist and velcro tabs, into which you insert the cloth nappy. If the idea of washing nappies puts you off, there are nappy-washing services which will pick up and return your nappies – all for the same cost as buying disposables.

● **Disposable nappies might be convenient,** but they are more expensive, financially and environmentally, than cloth nappies. Most are bleached, a process that yields, as a by-product, highly toxic dioxins, which have been linked to cancer. Most contain fragrances and polyacrylate crystals or gel (to increase absorbency), which are possible irritants to infants. Finally, their disposal presents major environmental problems: they are often made of non-biodegradable plastics and millions are thrown away each year and end up in landfill.

Never allow children to use solvent-based glues: they give off toxic fumes. White, water-based PVA glues are a safe choice.

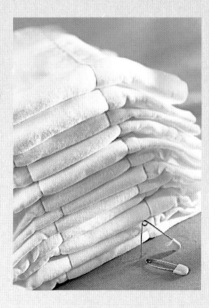

● **If you feel you can't do without disposable nappies,** try to find non-bleached, non-gel, natural cotton or wood-pulp ones. You might also consider a nappy system of disposable pads held inside washable pants – these are non-bleached, non-perfumed, non-plastic and compostable.

Pens and permanent markers

● **Many felt-tipped permanent marker pens** are solvent based, and some contain xylene and/or toluene, which have been linked to damage to the nervous system, kidneys and liver. A strong odour usually indicates a chemical solvent. Permanent markers that use alcohol as a solvent are safer.

● **If you need a permanent pen,** choose a fine-tip not a broad-tip, as less solvent is released on to the paper.

● **A better option is to choose a non-permanent pen,** marked 'water-based' or 'non-toxic'.

Plastic wrap

● **Most plastic wraps are made from polyethylene,** but chemical plasticisers are added to some commercial wrappings to make them pliable. Many of these chemicals, including phthalates and adipates, are toxic and can leach into food. Try to avoid using plastic wrap for storing food.

● **Rewrap food in plastic wrapping,** particularly cheese or other fatty foods, in waxed or greaseproof paper.

Sanitary protection

● **Look for 100 per cent organic cotton tampons or pads,** or for cotton pads that are unbleached, or bleached with hydrogen peroxide or oxygen bleach, not chlorine.

● **Try reusable pads.** Made from 100 per cent soft cotton fabric, in various thicknesses, they can be used for menstruation or incontinence. See the internet for suppliers.

Shaving products

● **Look for non-aerosol, fragrance-free, soap-based** shaving creams.

● **The petroleum derivative isopropyl alcohol** is often used in aftershaves and toners. Consider plant-based alternatives containing witch hazel, rosewater, lemon grass, chamomile, cucumber or peppermint (effective for oily skin).

Sunscreen

● **Although the toxic PABAs have now been eliminated** from most sunscreens, almost all still contain potentially harmful chemicals, including diethanolamine,

MOBILE PHONES

There are well over 65 million mobile phones in use in the UK and the majority of owners upgrade their phone every couple of years or so. If discarded phones are sent to landfill sites, the batteries and circuit boards break down, releasing nickel and other metals into the soil and groundwater.

When disposing of a mobile phone, make sure that you have it recycled. There are numerous recycling programmes to choose from, many linked to charities. Check the internet for details.

......**woolly choice**..........................
Choose pure **wool blankets.** Wool is
**warm, comfortable and naturally
fire-resistant,** and emits no harmful fumes.

triethanolamine and the parabens, and benzophenone, which can interfere with reproductive cycles and is thought to increase the risk of certain cancers.

• **The safest options are the physical UV-blockers** zinc oxide and titanium dioxide, a hat and protective clothing.

Tea

• **Buy loose-leaf tea and use a teapot** or a stainless steel infuser, or look for unbleached natural-fibre tea bags.

• **Try to avoid tea grown using chemical pesticides and fertilisers.** Look out for certified organic teas.

• **Herbal teas aren't necessarily a healthy alternative,** as the herbs are often grown in soil-free conditions in glasshouses, and doused with chemicals before and after harvest. If possible, choose a certified organic herbal tea.

Tinned food

• **It is not yet known whether the material** used to line food cans (an epoxy resin containing the hormone disruptor Bisphenol A) leaches into the food in dangerous amounts.

• **Try to avoid canned baby foods,** as babies are more susceptible to minute amounts of any chemical. Look for baby food in glass containers instead.

• **Use canned food sensibly:** rotate the cans in your larder so that the oldest items are used first, and watch the use-by date. Never heat food directly in the can.

Tissues and toilet paper

• **It's hard to believe** that toilet paper could contain formaldehyde, artificial fragrance and dye, but it often does. Look for undyed, unbleached, fragrance-free tissues and toilet paper made from recycled paper.

Toothcare products

• **Some toothpastes and over-the-counter mouthwashes** may contain triclosan. It reacts with chlorine in water to form chloroform and is not readily biodegradable.

• **Look in your health food shop for toothpaste** that is made from natural ingredients, or simply use bicarbonate of soda on a soft toothbrush. For a mouthwash, try rinsing with water and a few drops of clove or peppermint essential oil.

Wine

• **In conventional viticulture,** fungicides, insecticides and herbicides are applied to grape vines. After harvesting, winemakers use preservatives (usually sulphur dioxide or sulfites), which can cause allergic reactions.

• **If you are concerned about additives,** seek out certified organic wines (which contain a minimum level of preservatives) or wines labelled preservative-free. Bear in mind that the latter may not keep well long term.

To reduce waste, **avoid one-piece disposable razors.** Choose a quality razor with a **disposable blade** instead

Waste watch

Reduce, reuse and recycle: adopt this simple three-pronged approach and you'll be surprised how much you'll save and how little you'll waste.

Reduce and reuse

Choosing products with little or no packaging is an easy way to reduce what comes into your home and what ends up in landfill. Reusing instead of throwing away makes economic sense – not only that, devising ingenious ways to reuse household items is fun. And whatever you put out for recycling will find its way back to you in other products.

Minimising waste

● Try to use paper rather than plastic bags when packing fruit and vegetables for weighing, and where possible avoid pre-packed produce.

● Make sure you always take reusable bags with you when shopping and refuse plastic carrier bags.

● Look for products that have minimum or recyclable packaging, or that come in refillable and/or returnable

Schools and children's centres can make use of a variety of discarded goods for craft and play activities. Egg cartons and cardboard tubes from paper towels are always popular.

containers. Some health food shops and farm shops even encourage customers to bring their own containers.

● **Choose reusable products,** such as rechargeable batteries, rather than the disposable alternatives.

Reusing materials

Many items that are normally consigned to the garbage bin can be modified to serve all kinds of useful purposes.

PAPER PRODUCTS
● **Roll used giftwrap around empty cardboard tubes** to keep it crease-free, ready for the next time you need to wrap a present, or use it to line shelves or drawers.

● **Make your own gift tags:** cut motifs from giftwrap or pictures from old greetings cards and glue them to cards.

● **Open out paper carrier bags and decorate with a stamp** or potato print to make wrapping paper.

● **Clip or staple your scrap paper into notepads** to keep by the phone or in the kitchen.

● **Make sure you use both sides of the paper in your printer** or fax machine before recycling.

● **Use old newspapers as a lining** for your pet's basket or kennel (they can be easily and cheaply replaced) and to line your kitchen garbage bin, instead of plastic bags.

● **Use sheets of old newspaper for cleaning windows,** greasy pans and barbecues, as well as for wrapping food scraps that can't go in the compost.

CARTONS, JARS AND CANS
● **Use an egg carton or cut-down milk carton** with drainage holes cut in the bottom for seed propagation. Once the seedlings are big enough, plant the carton or each detached 'egg cup' directly in the ground. The carton will protect the seedling, then biodegrade and disappear.

Shredded newspaper makes a useful mulch for the garden, and you can add it (in moderation) to your compost bin.

make it
yourself

A simple Chinese lantern

clean can
pen
sharp craft knife
spray paint (optional)
wire, 0.9 mm

Mark two lines around a clean empty can, about 2.5cm from the top and bottom.

With a sharp craft knife, make vertical cuts about 1.5cm apart between the lines. Make a cut across the bottom of two adjacent strips to make an opening for a candle.

Gently press down on the can to make the strips bend in the middle. Insert a tea-light through the opening, then tuck the cut ends of the opening strips inside the can.

Finally, attach a hanging loop.

You can also spray paint the can before cutting if you like to make lanterns in different colours.

- **Wash plastic milk and juice containers** thoroughly and use them to freeze soups and sauces.

- **Use old juice and dairy cartons** as peel-away moulds for home-made soap and candles.

- **Fill plastic smoothie or probiotic drink bottles with water or sand** and use to play indoor skittles.

- **Use old yoghurt cartons to plant out seedlings,** or cut them into strips to use as plant labels.

- **Save glass jars and bottles for preserving,** jam making and pickling.

- **Refill pretty or unusual-shaped glass bottles** with home-made herb oil or vinegar for gifts.

- **Keep airtight glass jars for storing herbs, rice and pulses.** The foods benefit from being stored this way, and you can see at a glance what's inside.

- **Use glass jars for salad dressings** and leftover sauce. It's easier to clean these liquids out of glass than plastic.

- **Cut the top half off a plastic soft drink bottle** and use it to clear leaves from your gutters. Or place it over seedlings to protect them from the frost and birds.

- **The bottom part of a soft drink bottle** makes a handy paint container when painting woodwork or window frames.

- **Use herb and spice jars** for storing items such as elastic bands, safety pins, paper clips, nails and screws.

Buy **adhesive address labels** so that you can **reuse envelopes** that are still in good condition

TURNING OLD INTO NEW

For lots of clever ideas on reusing household items, check the internet. Here are a few to get you started.

- Running out of skirt hangers? Attach two clothes pegs (hinged) at either end of a coathanger.

- Use polystyrene trays as drip catchers for oily bottles.

- Reuse empty squeeze detergent bottles for storing home-made cleaning products, or to water indoor plants.

- Remove the lids from cans and convert them into hanging pots for epiphytes (air plants) or spring bulbs.

- Make a hole in the lid of an empty coffee can, pop a ball of string inside and thread the end out through the hole for tangle-free use.

- Small, empty vegetable oil cans can be turned into attractive pots for holding cooking utensils.

- Store items such as photos and receipts in old shoeboxes.

- Cut off the legs of old pairs of tights and use for securing plants to stakes – they won't cut into the plant stem.

- If you've gathered lots of old tights, use them to stuff cushions and toys.

- Use an empty film canister to hold a travel sewing kit.

- **Use small cans to make attractive candle holders** for the garden or a city balcony.

CLOTHES AND FABRICS
Clothes, bedding, towels and curtains that have seen better days can be put to good use or given a new lease of life.

- **Save old shirts** to wear for gardening or when you are painting.

- **Socks that are past darning** come in handy as polishing cloths, padding for the ends of ladders, cobweb dusters (fitted over brooms) and for protecting stored valuables.

- **Turn odd socks into hand puppets** to amuse young children: just sew on buttons for the nose and eyes and some wool for hair. You could also use a small smiling upturned zip to make the mouth.

- **Cut off the legs of well-worn trousers** to make a pair of gardening shorts.

- **Remove the wires from an old electric blanket** and use the blanket as an underlay on your bed.

- **Sheets that are beyond saving and faded curtains** make good protective covers when decorating.

- **Sew discarded curtains into bags** for storing good coats, suits and dresses.

Save fabric scraps for patchwork quilting – baby blankets, pot holders, teacosies, bags, or even a full-size bedspread.

..... more for less ....
Cut down soft, thinning cotton sheets and towels for your child to use. A double sheet can provide six crib sheets.

Recycling

The best kind of recycling is giving things you don't want to someone who really needs them. The next best is making sure that any waste that can be recycled is separated from other rubbish ready for collection. In the UK over 60 per cent of packaging is recycled.

Pass it on

● **Go online** Use Freecycle, a web-based facility that puts people in touch with each other at a local level, to give away items you don't need (the recipient collects them). Or, to sell an item you no longer want, try the online auction Ebay.

● **Old spectacles can be donated to people in need overseas.** Ask your optician for information.

● **Doctors' and hospital waiting rooms** often need magazines and children's toys or books.

● **Charity shops** will recycle clothes, toys, books and household items, but not electrical goods.

● **Many charities will take furniture that is in good condition.** Or look up details of furniture recyclers in your local area on the internet.

● **Several charities use old greetings cards** to make new ones, which they then resell.

● **Old school textbooks can be donated,** via various charities, to children in the developing world.

● **Beekeepers and people who sell jam at markets** or school fetes are always on the lookout for jars.

● **Vets and pet shops will sometimes accept old newspapers** to shred and use as animal bedding.

● **Charities collect clothes, bedding and other textiles** to sell for funds, distribute to people in need or turn into rags that they sell to industry.

Hazardous waste

Some items are recyclable but contain heavy metals or toxic chemicals that must be handled with care and disposed of carefully. Find out what can be recycled and how to do it from your council or use the internet.

good eggs!
Stallholders at growers' markets are often happy to receive old egg cartons, which they reuse for fresh eggs.

RECYCLING CHECKLIST

Most local governments operate a recycling service. Many also offer additional disposal services and can supply information about companies that can take the waste that they are unable to deal with. Always check with your own council what they will take. Rinse out bottles, jars, cans and milk cartons before leaving them out.

CAN BE RECYCLED

✓ Glass jars and bottles: remove lids

✓ Paper: newspapers, magazines, telephone directories (sometimes there's a special collection), envelopes, computer paper, paper packaging, cardboard, pizza boxes (not accepted by all councils)

✓ Steel cans

✓ Steel aerosol cans

✓ Steel jam jar lids

✓ Metal bottle tops

✓ Aluminium cans

✓ Aluminium foil (not accepted by all councils)

✓ Milk and fruit juice cartons (not accepted by all councils)

✓ PET, HDPE and PVC plastics: check which types your council accepts; remove lids

✓ Green waste: but try to use in compost or a wormery instead

CANNOT BE RECYCLED

✗ Plastic bags (some large supermarkets provide bins to collect these for recycling)

✗ Oven-proof, window or mirror glass

✗ Food wrappers

✗ Facial tissues

✗ Polystyrene food or beverage containers

✗ Wax-coated cardboard

✗ Cellophane and foil giftwrap

✗ Plastic-covered paper

✗ Drinking glasses

✗ Light bulbs

✗ Ceramics

SORTING WITH CARE

If unrecyclable items are mixed with recyclable ones, the batch becomes useless, so it's important to sort your recycling carefully. A single piece of a ceramic cup, for example, can make a tonne of glass unusable.

● Take the caps off all bottles.

● Separate rubber bands and plastic wrap from paper.

● Remove the plastic cap and nozzle from steel aerosol cans, but do not attempt to crush them.

● Some councils require you to remove the plastic window from window envelopes before recycling.

● Squash cans before recycling. You can buy a device called a 'Crush-a-Can' which will flatten them for you.

SAFE DISPOSAL

Some things cannot be recycled but do require thoughtful disposal to avoid contaminating the environment or harming others.

✓ Ask your pharmacist how to dispose of out-of-date medicines and other drugs. Do not throw them into the garbage or flush them down the toilet.

✓ Check with your local council before you throw out the miscellaneous old cans and bottles in your garage or garden shed. Many of them are likely to contain hazardous chemicals.

✓ If you have decided to get rid of all the toxic cleaning products in your laundry and kitchen, don't simply throw them into the garbage. Contact your local council for information on disposal.

● **Ask if your council takes car and household batteries** for recycling. Many batteries contain heavy metals such as lead, zinc and cadmium. Some retailers recycle batteries.

● **Drain used motor oil into a clean container** and take it to your local garage or council depot for recycling.

● **Find out if paint cans can be included** with domestic waste or if they have to be taken to the depot separately.

● **Ask at mobile phone shops** if they will accept your old mobile phone for recycling.

● **Recycle used printer ink and toner cartridges** and buy recycled replacements, to help the environment, save money and in some cases help a charity. Consult the internet for details.

● **Relatively new computers can be given to charities;** older models can be recycled for parts. Consult the internet.

● **White goods and electrical appliances** can be returned to electrical retailers who are now obliged by law, under the WEEE (Waste Electrical and Electronic Equipment) directive to recycle them. They are also accepted by most local councils.

● **Most councils offer information** about where you can take a car to be recycled safely.

● **Rubber tyres can be recycled into new products.** Contact your local council or tyre dealer.

● **To recycle scrap metal,** check with your council or in the Yellow Pages.

Recycling food and garden waste

Don't throw food scraps down the sink. Instead recycle them on the compost heap to help fertilise your garden. Make your own compost using alternate layers of carbon-rich 'brown' materials – straw, hay, dried leaves, sawdust and shredded newspaper, and torn-up cardboard – with layers of nitrogen-rich 'green' materials – animal manures, grass clippings, fresh leaves, tea bags, coffee grounds and vegetable peelings. (See page 112 for information on building a compost heap.)

● **Don't add too much of any one material** to compost or the process of decomposition will slow down.

● **Don't compost meat, grease, cooking oil and dairy products** – see the checklist opposite.

● **A wormery is ideal if you have limited space** to build a compost heap as it is small enough to be kept on a balcony. It is an ideal way to recycle kitchen waste and

..... food watch ....
More than one-third of all food bought in the UK is thrown away – of which half is edible.

produces very fertile compost. See page 112 for more information on wormeries.

● **Feed the worms** vegetable and fruit scraps, tea bags, coffee grounds, crushed eggshells, old grass clippings and manure.

● **Don't feed the worms** meat, dairy products, fat, onions, garlic, banana skins, or too much citrus or spicy food.

COMPOSTING CHECKLIST

Most biodegradable materials can be put onto the compost heap, but careful screening of scraps will produce better results. The greater the variety of ingredients, the better the compost. For the best results, chop up coarse materials.

WHAT TO PUT IN

✓ Fruit and vegetable peelings and cores – great for getting compost started

✓ Cooked table scraps

✓ Coffee grounds – supply proteins and oils

✓ Tea-leaves and unbleached tea bags – add welcome nitrogen

✓ Old bread

✓ Eggshells

✓ Shredded newspaper – in small amounts

✓ Wood shavings, sawdust or fire ash

✓ Household dust and hair

✓ Garden waste – leaves, non-woody prunings, grass

WHAT TO LEAVE OUT

✗ Fats and oils

✗ Meat and bones – take too long to break down and can attract pests

✗ Citrus peel – fine in small quantities, but contains a preservative that can inhibit decomposition

✗ Corn cobs – take too long to decompose

✗ Salt

✗ Anything that has been treated with chemicals

✗ Weed seeds

✗ Diseased plant material

✗ Dog or cat faeces

the earth-wise garden

Look after your soil, choose plants that suit your climate and situation, use water wisely and try organic methods before resorting to chemicals, and your earth-wise garden will reward you with healthy plants and produce all year round. If you work with nature, you'll also find that your garden is easier and cheaper to maintain. It's the secret to a successful garden.

A natural garden

An eco-friendly garden makes the most of an existing site and is easier and cheaper to maintain. Work with nature and you'll be richly rewarded.

Getting started

When it comes to garden design, don't be tempted to throw out the old and bring in the new. Understanding and accommodating the limitations of your particular site will save time, money and effort and will increase your chances of success over the long term.

Keep it simple

● **Develop what is already in your garden,** rather than try to change it. If your land is poorly drained, for example, instead of installing an expensive drainage system, think about planting a bog garden. If possible, witness your garden throughout a year before making radical changes.

Let nature take over in a corner of your garden. Wild plants lend a natural beauty and don't require chemical fertilisers or weedkillers.

• **Observe and record the names of plants** that thrive in your area – and the ones that don't. Rather than visiting show gardens, seek out overgrown areas and gardens with mature plants to identify plants that will survive on neglect.

• **Get rid of plants that continually struggle to survive.** If you don't have a sunny aspect, stop hankering for tender agapanthus and learn to love shade-loving acanthus. If your lawn isn't getting enough light or there's too much root competition under trees, replace the grass with a groundcover that tolerates shade.

• **Before buying a plant, find out about its growth habit,** including its mature height and width, and plant accordingly, otherwise it will need a lot of maintenance.

• **Mimic nature by covering the soil with organic mulch.** As well as providing regular nourishment to the soil and suppressing weeds, mulch keeps the soil cool and reduces moisture loss.

• **Don't persevere with poor soil.** If your soil is clay-based, and you've struggled unsuccessfully for years to improve it, build raised beds of good-quality soil on top of it.

The fundamentals

No matter what type of garden you have or choose there are three basic requirements.

• **Sun and shade.** South-facing means sunny and north-facing means shady. Choose the best places for your garden beds, lawns and outdoor living areas according to their aspect.

• **Shelter from strong wind** is essential for plant growth and for your own comfort. If your garden is exposed, plant according to the wind direction. Create a multi-layered windbreak with tall plants facing the prevailing winds and layers of lower plants facing the area you wish to shelter.

• **Healthy soil.** The composition of the earth in your garden – whether it is sand, clay or loam – and its depth, drainage patterns, pH and nutrient levels will determine what you can grow, although applying nutrient-rich mulches and organic matter can improve many unpromising sites (see page 110).

Golden outdoor rules

• **Use a broom, not a hose,** to clean hard surfaces. A regular sweep will prevent a build-up of mould-causing leaves, twigs and other organic debris. Keep a stiff heavy-duty broom solely for outdoor use.

• **Keep drainage grates free of leaves.**

• **Clear guttering and downpipes regularly.**

• **Store wooden garden furniture,** canvas chairs and umbrellas out of the weather, otherwise they will rot.

• **Ensure that the water in your water feature is clean.**

• **To prevent rusting,** put away garden tools after use.

• **Store your hose on a reel** to keep it neat and prevent kinks forming. It will work more efficiently and last longer.

MAKE YOUR TOOLS LAST

• After use, wipe secateur blades with an oily rag to remove any plant residue and protect from rust. Sterilise the blades by wiping them with methylated spirits.

• Sharpen secateurs and shears regularly: rub the cutting edge, round side down, with a sharpening stone dampened with water or oil. Blunt blades can damage plants. For ease of use, keep oil in a plunge dispenser bottle.

• To clean and protect against rust, after each use, plunge the metal parts of your tools into a bucket filled with 30cm sand mixed with a little lubricating oil.

• Buy polished stainless steel spades and forks: they are easier to use and clean, and don't rust.

Going organic

Many people are turning to organic gardening, which avoids the use of chemicals and restores the natural relationship between plants and the environment.

Eight guidelines for organic gardening

1 **Create healthy soil.** Add plenty of mulch and dig in organic matter. If you need help to start with, buy certified organic soil treatments and manures from your local nursery.

2 **Encourage biodiversity.** Plant a wide variety of species and intermingle them. See also companion planting, page 102.

3 **Rotate crops.** To conserve soil fertility and to reduce the build-up of diseases, don't grow the same annuals, plants and vegetables in the same place year after year.

4 **Understand the terrain.** Choose plants suitable for the soil, climate and aspect of your garden. Check the label stating soil preference when buying new plants.

5 **Use organic controls** so that natural pest predators can find their place in the garden. Don't use chemicals at the first sign of insect infestation, and learn to tolerate some damage to your plants. Over time, your garden will evolve into a balanced and rewarding ecosystem.

IMPROVE YOUR SOIL

● First find out what type of soil you have and if it is alkaline, neutral or acidic (see page 109).

● To improve soil fertility and structure, apply well-rotted compost and manure each year.

● Protect areas of bare soil from the elements by growing green manure. See box page 114.

● The leaves of comfrey contain abundant potash which makes an ideal liquid manure. Weigh the cut leaves from six plants and place them in a large bucket. Pour over 22.5 litres of water to every 1.6kg of leaves and cover. When the leaves have decomposed, strain off the liquid and use undiluted on your plants.

● If necessary, use a compound organic fertiliser such as blood, fish and bone meal.

Ensure success by choosing plants to suit the conditions in your garden. In acid soil and semi-shade, grow rhododendrons.

6 **Learn to distinguish** between friends and foes. Never assume that an insect or other creature that appears in your garden for the first time is the scout of an invading army. It is much more likely to be a friend that has come to protect you from invasion and to enjoy the safety of your pesticide-free garden.

7 **Make sure that you adopt the organic system** throughout your garden – vegetable garden, herbaceous borders, lawns and paths.

8 **Accept that in nature nothing is perfect,** that some untidiness is natural and that mistakes and losses are an inevitable part of achieving a natural balance in your garden.

Organic strategies

As an organic gardener, you don't have to sit back and do nothing when your plants are attacked by animals, birds and insects. If you have been using pesticides in your garden up to now, you should expect some losses at first. However, in time the following organic strategies will prove effective and rewarding.

● **Choose plant varieties that are resistant to disease** – they will survive problems that might prove fatal to less robust plants.

● **Walk around the garden every day** to check for problems. Tackling pests and diseases at the first sign of trouble will give you a head start.

● **Remove the pests you can see by hand.** In the first stages of infestation, this method works especially well for leaf-munching caterpillars, snails and slugs.

● **Drape lightweight netting over vegetables and fruit** to protect them from birds and other small animals. Check the netting daily to make sure nothing is trapped in it.

● **While they are becoming established,** protect young trees and shrubs from larger animals by circling them with wire netting or sturdy plastic.

● **To protect plants at risk from slugs and snails** surround them with wood ash, sawdust, crushed eggshells, blood and bone or lime.

● **Prevent damage to ripening fruit** by covering it with a cloth or waxed paper bag. This is a great way to stop birds eating tomatoes, peaches or figs.

● **Encourage birds and beneficial insects,** such as beetles and parasitic wasps, into your garden to establish natural pest and disease control by growing plants such as lavender, thyme and rosemary. These will provide them with food, shelter and breeding places.

A garden that's free of pesticides is kinder to all living organisms and costs much less to maintain

Inspect shoots and leaves regularly for signs of disease and pick off any pests that you see.

...... **good riddance** ....

Your first step in an organic garden is to
safely dispose of any chemicals
in your shed. Ask your local council for details.

Natural pest repellents

Choose plants that suit your growing conditions and you'll have fewer problems with plant-damaging pests. But at times plants will need a helping hand. Common pests are easily deterred by simple, natural methods that won't harm the beneficial insects in your garden.

Natural pest control

● **Inspect plants regularly,** remembering to check the undersides of leaves.

● **Remove pests by hand** and either squash them, or drop them into a bucket containing water and a little detergent.

● **Use diversity as a strategy against plant pests.** Intermingle different types of plants to avoid providing pests with a banquet of their one favourite food. See also companion planting, page 102.

● **Check seedlings or cuttings from other gardeners** as you could be importing pests into your garden.

● **Encourage beneficial insects such as hoverflies** and spiders into your garden by avoiding the use of pesticides.

● **Welcome useful insects** such as ladybirds and lacewings, which feed on aphids and other pests. Grow sunflowers, marigolds, asters, wild carrots or fennel to encourage these beneficial insects into your garden.

● **Collect and dispose of any infested and rotten fruit** as it may harbour pest eggs. Do not compost.

Aphids

These sap-sucking pests can cause severe damage in the garden. They stunt plant growth, spread viral diseases and excrete a sugary waste that encourages sooty mould.

Use netting and seedbed covers to deter thieving birds, or string up glinting CDs to scare them off

SAFER SPRAYS FOR THE ORGANIC GARDENER

Most chemicals should be avoided in the organic garden, but there are some sprays that are approved for use – even though they may also kill beneficial insects.

Ingredient	Origin	Problems controlled
Copper	Naturally occurring element	Diseases including potato blight and damping off
Pyrethrum	Made from the flowers of *Tanacetum cinerariifolium*	Wide range of pests including aphids and caterpillars
Quassia	Derived from the bark of a tree, *Picrasma quassioides*	Many leaf pests, especially aphids
Rotetone (derris)	Made from powdered roots of various tropical plants	Wide range of pests, including aphids, caterpillars, sawfly and thrips
Soaps	Made from organic fatty acids	Wide range of pests, including aphids, red spider mite and whitefly
Sulphur	Naturally occurring element	Fungus diseases (may damage some plants)

● **Aphids infest the new shoots of plants,** causing distorted leaves. Hose them off or squash with your fingers.

● **Whitefly larvae also suck sap,** resulting in mottled and papery leaves. Use yellow sticky cards to trap the flies.

● **Scale can be kept under control** by its natural predators, which include lacewing larvae.

Snails and slugs

● **One of the best ways to deal with snails and slugs** is to walk around the garden with a torch at night, when they are at their most active (particularly after it has been raining), and squash any that you see.

● **Get rid of rough, weedy areas,** piles of rocks and rubbish. Snails and slugs shelter and breed in these places.

● **Place empty grapefruit halves,** with little doorways cut into them, near threatened plants. Slugs and snails will be attracted to the beer and congregate inside the grapefruit halves, ready for collection and disposal in the morning.

● **Snails and slugs dislike crossing rough surfaces.** Put physical barriers – such as sawdust, grit or crushed eggshells – around plants.

● **Surround plants with copper strips.** Copper reacts with the mucus secreted by slugs and snails, creating an electrical charge.

Leaf-eaters

● **When removing caterpillars from your plants,** look for clusters of eggs on the undersides of leaves and destroy them before they have a chance to hatch into a second generation of caterpillars.

● **Encourage birds to come into your garden** by putting nesting boxes in trees (see pages 104-105). The birds and their young will eat caterpillars by the thousand.

Snails and slugs find it difficult to resist bowls of stale beer or fermented fruit juice or milk. They dive straight in and drown.

THE EARTH-WISE GARDEN

Companion planting

By mixing complementary plants you employ the tactics used by plants themselves to survive. They will act as allies to entice, deter or confuse pests, or provide neighbouring plants with protection from the sun, wind, frost and weeds.

● **Plant French marigolds** (*Tagetes*) to get rid of nematodes (soil-borne pests that infest the root systems of plants). They don't like the chemicals that the marigolds exude from their roots.

● **Confuse the enemy** by mixing a variety of plants together. A plethora of different aromas can put insects off the scent of their favourite foods.

● **Use strong-smelling herbs,** such as lavender and tansy, as a mask for the more delicate scents of other crops and herbs. This strategy will keep them free of sap-sucking pests, such as aphids.

● **Disguise your vegetables and herbs** by introducing differently shaped plants into your vegetable patch. This will fool some insect pests that seem to recognise their food sources by shape. Cabbage white butterflies, for example, are thought to be drawn to the round shape of cabbages.

● **Allow some of your vegetables to mature** to the flowering stage. The flowers of broccoli, cabbages, cauliflowers and other brassicas are favourite foods for aphids and cabbage white butterflies.

● **Some plants, such as peas and beans,** are nitrogen-fixers – they convert nitrogen from the atmosphere into soil-enriching nitrogen compounds. Plant them with a crop that thrives on extra nitrogen, such as corn-on-the-cob.

● **Include plants that provide a safe haven** for beneficial insects when times are tough. Many of these insects need a source of nectar and pollen to survive while they are waiting for the pests to arrive.

● **Plant aromatic flowering species** close to crops that need pollinating, to attract bees.

● **Plant a mixture of tall and low-growing vegetables** in the same patch. This is an ideal way of making the most of the available space. For example, plant French beans with tomatoes or round-headed garden lettuces with leeks.

TRADITIONAL COMBINATIONS

Plant	Companion	Benefits
Apples	Chives	Reduce fungal diseases
Cabbages	Nasturtiums	Attract caterpillars away
Carrots	Leeks	Repel carrot and onion flies
Roses	Lavender	Repel aphids
Strawberries	Garlic/onions	Protect from grey mould
Tomatoes	French marigolds	Repel greenfly and blackfly

HERB REPELLENTS

The following herbs exude volatile oils that repel the insects listed. Grow these herbs to keep away pests and as barrier plants to protect other plants.

● **Basil** – flies
● **Camomile** – flies
● **Dill** – cabbage moth
● **Fennel** – fleas
● **Marigold** – nematodes, aphids
● **Mint** – cabbage moth
● **Nasturtium** – ants, aphids
● **Pennyroyal** – ants
● **Rue** – flies
● **Sage** – cabbage moth
● **Tansy** – ants

Keeping weeds in check

Not all weeds are a nuisance – some can be useful by covering ground which would otherwise be exposed. However, aggressive weeds should be eradicated. Here are several effective non-chemical control methods.

Weed control

• **Don't bring weeds into your garden.** Avoid importing soil, including topsoil, that may contain weed seeds or pieces. Check for weeds in the pots of new plants.

• **Avoid leaving areas of soil bare** for a long period or weeds will soon colonise them. Hoe bare soil regularly, ideally while weed seedlings are small and the soil is dry. This will deprive weeds of nutrients and moisture.

• **Cover weeded areas with mulch** to prevent weed seeds germinating. Remove any new weeds as they appear.

• **Remove weeds before they flower.** Mow annual weeds to remove flower heads and seeds.

• **Smother weeds with a thick layer of newspaper** or cardboard and cover with mulch, then plant through the mulch and paper, keeping the soil covered.

• **Cover larger areas of weedy ground** with heavy-duty black polythene, weighed down with bricks, or a woven mesh weed mat.

• **Digging brings dormant weed seeds to the soil surface** so a couple of weeks after digging, check the site and hoe off any small seedlings that have developed.

• **With persistent weeds remove the whole root** and all underground parts. Some weeds regrow from a tiny piece.

• **In warm, dry weather,** leave small uprooted weeds on top of the soil to dry out but never leave weeds lying on moist ground, where they may continue to ripen and seed.

Dandelions have very long tap roots so make sure you remove the whole root when you weed

To suppress weed growth, plant through a semi-permeable membrane and cover with a layer of mulch.

The wildlife garden

Hedgehogs, frogs, toads and birds feed on many pests that attack plants. Ladybirds devour aphids. Butterflies and bees pollinate flowers – and earthworms are vital for fertile soil. Welcome them all into your garden.

Birds

● **Many garden birds eat pests.** For example, blue tits eat caterpillars and aphids; starlings prey on grubs; sparrows, great tits and wrens consume insects; while song thrushes eat snails and slugs. They are attracted to gardens on the edges of woodlands and where there is water.

● **Plant hedges** such as alder, viburnum and shrub roses. Their thick-branched growth hides and protects nests.

● **Encourage birds into the garden** by growing plants that bear berries, such as elderberry, pyracantha and viburnum and those that bear seeds, such as ornamental grasses and sunflowers.

● **Install a bird table in your garden.** Ideally, buy one that has a roof and a rim around the edge to prevent seeds from falling to the ground. As a deterent to predators, fit a circular piece of wood to the post about 30cm beneath the table top.

● **Never put out raw meat or mouldy bread** and never offer desiccated coconut as it may swell in a bird's crop and cause it to choke.

● **Avoid putting out too much food** when trying to attract birds into the garden – uneaten seeds will quickly become damp and mouldy.

● **Refill birdbaths at least once a day.** Place a few stones in the water for the birds to stand on and position the birdbath in full sun but out of reach of potential predators.

Ladybird larvae and other beneficial insect predators can be bought from specialist suppliers, often listed in gardening magazines

make it yourself

Building a nest box

Use only untreated wood. You will need: 12mm-thick wood for the roof and base, 23 x 28cm for the roof and 15 x 12cm for the base; 35 x 15cm of 12mm-thick wood for the back; 57cm of wood with the bark on, cut into 3 pieces 15cm wide for the sides and front. Fix the roof with a 15cm length of 12 x 12mm beading. Make the entrance hole 3cm in diameter.

1 Cut the bark wood in three pieces: one 15 x 16.5cm for the front and two 15 x 20cm for the sides, cut at an angle.

2 Bevel the top edge of the front section to match the sloping edges of the sides, then drill the entrance hole.

3 Glue the front and sides together, then screw in place. Fix on the back in the same way.

4 Fix the base section in the same way as the back. Screw on the roof and add beading to make the nest box watertight.

• **If you don't have a bird bath,** place a few shallow, flat-bottomed pot saucers on the ground and fill them with water.

• **Put nest boxes in your garden** to encourage tits which are partial to fruit tree pests. A 3cm diameter hole near the top will allow these birds in but will keep out sparrows. Place the box at least 1.5m from the ground, out of reach of predators. (See Building a nest box, opposite.)

Bees and butterflies

These feed on nectar and pollen from flowers, and in so doing pollinate numerous plants, particularly fruit trees, ensuring a good harvest.

• **Most butterflies will only lay their eggs** on plants that are in full sun, so if you want a garden of butterflies, provide them with generous clumps of stinging nettles in the sun.

• **Butterflies are attracted** by purple, orange, yellow and red flowers. Remember that nectar is more accessible to a butterfly in single than in double blooms (some of which may produce no nectar) and that butterflies find it hard to sip from flowers that hang down or have ruffled petal edges.

Ladybirds

Ladybirds are one of the gardener's best allies against insect pests, including aphids, scale insects and red spider mite. Encouraging them will reduce the need for other control measures. Colonies of ladybirds will build up in your garden and soon devour up to 50 aphids per day each.

• **Allow clumps of nettles to grow in your garden.** Nettles harbour an aphid that will not attack your other plants and is an excellent food source for ladybirds.

• **Ladybird larvae and beneficial insect predators** can be bought from specialist suppliers: consult the internet.

PLANTS TO ATTRACT WILDLIFE

FOR BIRDS
BERBERIS Shrubs with yellow or orange flowers in late spring and blue-black or red fruit in autumn.

COTONEASTER Shrubs with white flowers in late spring and early summer and red berries in autumn.

LONICERA PERICLYMENUM (honeysuckle) Deciduous climber with cream flowers in summer and autumn followed by red berries.

FOR BEES
ACHILLEA MILLEFOLIUM (yarrow) Perennial with white flat-topped clusters in late summer and autumn.

FILIPENDULA ULMARIA (meadowsweet) Perennial with large, creamy white flowers in mid summer.

FOR BUTTERFLIES
ASTER (Michaelmas daisy) Perennials with mauve, pink or white flowers in late summer and autumn.

AUBRIETA DELTOIDEA Evergreen perennial with violet to mauve, starry flowers in spring.

BUDDLEIA DAVIDII (butterfly bush) Deciduous shrub with purple spikes in late spring and summer.

WILDLIFE ALLIES IN THE GARDEN

GROUND BEETLES Scurrying, big black beetles that are more often seen at night. Both adults and their larvae are useful predators of slugs, caterpillars and aphids.

HOVERFLIES A group of true flies that look like bees and wasps. Their greeny brown larvae, 12mm long, feed on aphids and can eat up to 100 a day.

HEDGEHOGS They eat caterpillars, beetles and slugs at night. If they visit, put out tinned dog food, not milk. A log pile provides shelter and a place to hibernate.

ROVE BEETLES This group includes the distinctive looking devil's coach horse beetle (above). Both adults and larvae are active predators of soil grubs, insects and slugs.

LADYBIRDS A single larva can eat 500 aphids, so they are worth encouraging. Two-spot and seven-spot ladybirds are the most common.

WASPS Many solitary wasps are beneficial against aphids and caterpillars. Provide egg-laying sites by drilling 5-10mm holes in posts.

CENTIPEDES Fast-moving creatures, with one pair of legs per body segment, that eat all types of small insects. Don't confuse them with the slower millipedes, which feed on plant roots.

WORMS These pull organic matter into the soil, which saves you having to dig it in. They also open up the structure of the soil, aiding drainage and making it easier for plant roots to establish.

BATS Night feeders on nocturnal flying insects. Encourage them with bat boxes where they can roost. They are under threat, mainly because of poisons in the chemical treatment of roof timbers.

FROGS, TOADS AND NEWTS These amphibians prey on slugs, flies and other insects. They need a pond in which to breed and will return to it year after year.

LACEWINGS Adults are bright green and have large, see-through wings and long antennae. Both the adults and their larvae feed on aphids. You can buy chambers to protect them and lacewing eggs.

SLOW-WORMS These legless lizards up to 30cm long eat the small greyish slugs that feed on the soft growth of young plants and vegetables.

untidy friends

Don't keep your garden too tidy. Clearing up every corner is a sure way to discourage garden friends.

Frogs and toads

These eat insect pests and grubs that can damage plants.

● **Create a garden pond** which will provide a home for frogs, toads and aquatic insects. To speed up their arrival, put in some spawn from a nearby pond.

● **A pile of rocks set in leaf litter** in the corner of the garden will serve as a quiet and private hideaway for toads.

Earthworms

Earthworms bury and digest plant waste, drain the soil by digging tunnels, and strengthen soil structure.

● **Encourage worms to take up residence** by keeping the soil in your garden moist, mulched and manured.

● **Don't cut up worms.** Work in the middle of the day, when they are deeper in the soil, and use a fork, not a spade.

● **Enlist the help of worms** to keep fruit trees free from scab, a fungus disease that causes black or brown blotches on the leaves and fruit of apples and pears. The fungus grows on dead leaves and releases its spores at Christmas time. Run a mower over the leaves in autumn to chop them small. Worms can then easily pull them underground before the scab spores have a chance to infect healthy trees.

Hedgehogs

These are great devourers of slugs, snails, worms, insects, and small vertebrates, which they hunt at dusk.

● **Allow hedgehogs safe access to a pond** or a large saucer filled with water. Do not put out milk for hedgehogs – it is not good for them.

● **Leave a pile of leaves in a corner** of the garden to provide temporary shelter for hedgehogs during cold snaps.

● **Provide a shelter for hedgehogs in the winter,** which they can also use as a hiding place for the rest of the year. Pile up logs and branches, 30–50cm high, taking care to leave an entrance and a cavity in the centre. Line the cavity with dry leaves. Make sure that the retreat is positioned under the shelter of a leafy tree or against a sheltered wall: hedgehogs like to keep warm and dry.

MAKE A WILDLIFE POND

● Site a pond in an open, sunny position away from trees.

● Use a flexible sheet liner to make your pond – the sides of preformed plastic ponds are too steep and slippery for many creatures.

● Make a gently sloping beach of gravel or pile up some stones in one corner of the pond. This will allow easy and safe access for wildlife.

● Put aquatic plants, such as water lilies and water violets in the pond to oxygenate the water, shade it and provide extra routes in and out.

● Place a slender branch across one corner of the pond for birds to perch on to drink and dip into the water.

To encourage hedgehogs, put out bowls of water and food, such as muesli mixed with water, nuts, sultanas, cake with honey drizzled over it, and cat or dog food.

Garden basics

The first rule in the garden is to know your soil – the plants that thrive there will provide a clue. Then find out how to improve its composition and fertility.

Down to earth

A balanced, nutritious soil is essential for healthy plant growth. If you are not blessed with naturally fertile ground, there are several ways you can improve it.

Soil sense

● **Find out what type of soil you have.** Garden soils vary considerably. All are a mixture of ingredients such as clay, sand, limestone and humus, but proportions vary and one element may be strongly predominant (see box, opposite).

● **Work with the soil you have.** Replacement earth is expensive, difficult to import and may contain weed seeds.

● **Avoid adding lots of fertilisers** to soils that are poorly drained or too dry. Work on the drainage and soil structure first.

Improving the soil

Choosing plants that thrive in your soil type is a wiser strategy than trying to modify the soil to suit the plants you want to grow. Yet almost every soil type will benefit from the addition of organic compost or green manure.

Active earthworms in your garden beds are a **sign of healthy soil.** Worms add nitrogen to the soil and aerate it

SANDY SOILS

● **Dig in plenty of compost and well-rotted manure** before you start planting. Add more manure and organic mulch regularly to replenish nutrients and improve the soil's water-retention.

● **Dig in green manure on empty beds** (see page 114) and use as a surface mulch around plants to help to conserve water.

● **Line the base of a planting hole** with a few sheets of newspaper to slow water loss. Once the newspaper rots the root system should be well established.

● **Mix in a layer of loam or sandy loam** to improve the soil structure.

● **Add lime to correct the soil's acidity level** and improve its structure (lime helps to bind the sand particles).

CLAY

● **Dig in lime,** using a spade or a rotavator, to improve and break up the soil's heavy structure.

● **Add well-rotted organic matter,** such as compost and animal manure, to improve the drainage and aeration of the soil. Spread a 2-3cm layer over the surface and dig in well.

● **When planting shrubs and perennials in clay soil,** dig grit, sharp sand or granular organic matter such as fine-grade bark into the planting area to improve drainage.

CHALK OR LIME SOIL

● **Reduce the soil's alkalinity** by incorporating acidifying materials, such as well-rotted manure, garden compost or leaf mould.

● **Dig in well-rotted compost or manure liberally** and often to replenish nutrients and improve water retention.

Improving your soil will pay rich dividends. Whatever your soil type, it should be easy to dig, well aerated, able to retain moisture and fairly rich in nutrients.

IDENTIFYING YOUR SOIL

Using a spade, dig sample wedges from different areas (you may have more than one soil type) and look at the colour and texture.

SANDY SOIL: crumbly, gritty, pale coloured.

CLAY: light brown, yellow or grey; smooth, sticky and slippery when wet; forms clods.

CHALK OR LIME: yellowish-white; sticky to the touch but crumbly texture. Can be stony.

HUMUS-RICH SOIL: dark and friable with a smell of mushrooms.

Light, sandy soils are well aerated, easy to cultivate, and drain freely, but they dry out quickly and don't hold nutrients. Conversely, clay-based soils are dense, poorly aerated and heavy to dig. They retain nutrients and water and are prone to waterlogging. Most plants like conditions somewhere in between these extremes, so it's worth improving your soil balance and structure. The best, fertile, loamy soils are humus-rich and 20–25% clay, 30–35% lime or chalk and 40–50% sand.

ACID OR ALKALINE? To find out your soil's pH value – whether it is alkaline, neutral or acid – use a testing kit from a DIY or garden centre. Certain plants prefer either acid or alkaline soil, but most thrive on a neutral balance of about 6.5 pH.

Earth-friendly mulches

Mulches are a boon to gardeners as they improve the fertility of the soil, suppress weeds and conserve moisture. All organic material may be used as mulch in the garden, but try to use local materials.

Why mulch?

● **Organic mulches break down,** releasing nutrients into the soil. Inorganic mulches, such as pebbles, stabilise soil temperature in the root zone and help to prevent erosion.

● **Applying mulch to your garden is an inexpensive, easy and effective** way to reduce surface evaporation caused by wind and sun.

● **A layer of mulch works as a natural weed mat,** so there's no need for chemicals and time-consuming weeding.

TYPES OF MULCH

Organic mulch	Comments
Bark	Attractive, very durable and adds humus to the soil but contains no nutrients so plants will need feeding.
Coffee/tea grounds	Best used for azaleas and acid-loving plants in pots.
Compost	If using your own, make sure it's well rotted. Or, buy in bags or in bulk.
Garden prunings	Shred before using. Avoid diseased material or plants that have recently been sprayed with herbicides.
Grass clippings	Mix well with other materials or compost before use, as they can pack down into a water-shedding layer.
Manure	Age the manure, or compost it first.
Mushroom compost	May be alkaline, so check its pH before applying.
Weeds	Fresh, seed-free green weeds break down well in garden beds.

Organic mulch	Comments
Pine needles	Suitable around acid-loving plants such as azaleas and heathers. Slow to decompose.
Straw	A layer 10cm deep is recommended. Chopped straw helps to repel slugs and snails.
Wood chips	Cheaper than bark. Apply a high-nitrogen fertiliser before mulching young plants.

Living mulch	Comments
Groundcover plants	Suppress weeds; keep roots of other plants cool.

Inert mulch	Comments
Black polythene	Set out plants through slits cut in the plastic. Anchor the edges or bury in the soil.
Crushed bricks or roof tiles	Use for paths or around low water-using plants.
Gravel/pebbles	Easy to spread. Many forms are inexpensive.
Rocks	Decorative; excellent for keeping soil cool.

● **Mulch provides food and shelter** for insects and boosts the activity of worms and micro-organisms in the soil, which is good for plants.

Mulch from garden waste

● **If you have enough garden waste** to recycle regularly, buy a shredder and use disease-free prunings. If you only rarely have a lot of pruning to do, hire a shredder for a day and aim to produce enough mulch to last for months.

● **Run the lawnmower over leaves and small prunings** to make an instant mulch to collect and put on garden beds.

● **Collect fallen leaves in autumn** and put them straight on to garden beds. Store extra leaves in heaps to break down into leaf mould.

● **Start a compost heap** (see overleaf). Well-rotted compost makes an excellent mulch.

How to mulch

● **Apply mulch in late spring,** and keep it topped up throughout the year. The key is to avoid leaving any soil bare, so always mulch around new plantings straight away.

● **Prepare the ground.** Dig out all traces of perennial weeds, and water beds before and after applying mulch.

● **Spread mulch over the soil** and around the base of plants. Don't mound it around stems and trunks as it can cause rot. Aim for a depth of about 7.5–10cm.

● **If you use organic mulch,** add an organic fertiliser, such as chicken manure, because the mulch tends to rob the soil of nitrogen as it breaks down.

● **Mulch around fruit and vegetables,** such as strawberries and tomatoes, to keep the produce clean and help prevent soil-borne disease from attacking crops.

● **Prevent gravel mulch from spilling out** on to the lawn by installing a solid edge around all your garden beds.

When applying mulch to garden beds, first cover the plant with an upturned bucket or container to keep its leaves clean.

Apply mulch to the garden after rain or a thorough watering in order to retain moisture in the soil

To inhibit weed growth and conserve soil moisture, plant through slits in plastic sheeting and mulch around roots.

The compost heap

Plants derive most of their nutrients from compost, or decomposed organic matter in the soil. By adding extra compost to the soil you not only boost the health of your garden but, by recycling organic matter, you can reduce the waste going to landfill by up to 30 per cent.

If you're making a compost bin, build a four-sided structure that is at least 1 metre high and open at the top. Ensure one side is easy to remove so that you can turn the heap and remove finished compost.

Setting up

● **Work out the most convenient spot** in your garden for a compost heap. If possible, locate it fairly close to the kitchen, so that it is handy for the disposal of kitchen waste.

● **Use recycled materials** such as brick, stone, timber or plastic to make your compost bin. For example, an old plastic dustbin is an easy and inexpensive option. Simply cut out the bottom and press the bin into the soil. Keep the lid to cover it.

● **To aid drainage** and provide access to soil organisms, position the bin on a level, well-drained area so that it is in contact with the earth.

● **Make sure your compost heap** or bin is in the shade during the day because it shouldn't dry out too rapidly, nor should temperatures become so high that soil organisms can't survive.

Making your own

● **Alternate layers of carbon-rich 'brown' materials** – straw, hay, dried leaves, sawdust and shredded newspaper and cardboard – with layers of nitrogen-rich 'green' materials – animal manures, grass clippings, fresh leaves, prunings, tea bags, coffee grounds, and vegetable and fruit peelings. Try to keep the ratio of brown and green material roughly equal.

● **Don't compost** cooked food, dairy products or meat scraps (they attract rats), grease or cooking oil, dead animals, pet faeces, diseased plants or plant material treated with herbicides or other chemicals (see also Compost checklist, page 93).

● **Don't compost** invasive weeds that are going to seed. Although a hot compost heap will kill most seeds, it's best to be on the safe side and throw them out, or they'll spread through your compost then through your garden.

● **Use a shredder to chop up leaves** and thick prunings before adding them to the compost heap. Shredding helps to increase the surface area of the materials, making them more accessible to decomposing agents.

● **Don't use packaged compost 'accelerators'** or 'activators': they usually give a quick fix of nitrogen that won't last long and is of little benefit. Instead, use organic sources of nitrogen such as grass clippings or manure.

● **Add manures** such as horse, cow, goat, pig, sheep and chicken, but not dog and cat droppings – they may contain pathogens or wormicides. Age manure before adding it.

5 TIPS FOR TOP COMPOST

1 Turn the heap at least once a month, and more often, if possible, to accelerate the process.

2 Don't let it get too wet or too dry – it should be about as damp as a wrung-out sponge.

3 Too much of any one material will slow down or stop decomposition.

4 Try to maintain a balanced mix of brown and green material.

5 A good-sized heap generates enough heat for decomposition to occur. But if it is too big you won't be able to turn it properly to aerate it. The ideal size is about 1 x 1m.

make it yourself

Compost tea

Use this rich liquid fertiliser to water your plants or (diluted to about half strength) as a leaf spray.

Compost
1 bucket water
1 old sack

● Put the compost into an old porous sack.

● Immerse it in a bucket of water and leave for about 2 weeks.

● Remove the sack. Use the liquid as required.

● **If your compost needs a boost,** add a few shovelfuls of finished compost from the previous heap to speed the process. Manure and comfrey leaves are also good boosters. Or add a home-made liquid manure infusion made from 1 kilogram chopped nettles and 10 litres water (see page 114), turning the heap with a spade or fork to add air.

Composting autumn leaves

● **You can mix small amounts of leaves into the compost heap,** but large quantities are better stacked separately and left to break down into leaf mould.

● **Leaf mould is slower to make than compost** (it takes at least a year) but should need no attention after you have packed the leaves into netting cages or plastic bags.

● **Rake up fallen leaves after rain** and pack them into black plastic bags; tie the tops and punch a few holes in the sides with a garden fork. Stack the bags in a hidden corner of the garden for a year while the leaves decay into a rich crumbly mixture to use as a mulch around plants.

WORMERIES

A wormery is a simple, efficient way to convert kitchen waste into a concentrated liquid plant feed and a rich organic compost.

● Simply drop in your kitchen waste (for example, vegetable or fruit scraps, coffee grounds, tea bags) into the wormery and the worms will turn it into plant feed and compost.

● Wormeries can be bought at garden centres or on the internet.

● The best worms to use are tiger worms (Elsena fetida), which are available via the internet.

● It will take about 8 weeks for a wormery to produce liquid feed and about 6-8 weeks for a handful of waste to be converted into compost.

● The worms feed just below the top layer of food waste, so when the bin is full, remove the top few inches with a trowel, empty the compost and replace the top layer.

Gather autumn leaves for leaf mould and after a year you'll have a rich, crumbly mulch. Beech, chestnut and sycamore rot faster than oak, hornbeam and alder.

Feeding

To germinate, grow, flower and set seed, plants need certain essential elements. Some come from the air and water, but most are found in the soil. By adding organic fertilisers, it's possible to remedy nutrient deficiencies. Animal manures and seaweed are good natural fertilisers – and they are all either cheap or free.

How to use fertilisers

● **Always thoroughly water garden beds** before and after fertilising, or the fertiliser may damage plant roots. Conserve water and save money by fertilising your garden during periods of heavy rain.

● **Fertilise plants in the warmer months of the year,** when they are actively growing. In the cooler months they are dormant and don't need much food. Fertilise lawns twice a year, during spring and autumn.

● **Follow the directions on the container** – some plants, such as ferns, only require half-strength applications.

● **Learn which plants need plenty of fertiliser.** These 'gross' feeders include roses, lawns and most vegetables.

● **Slow-release fertilisers** are safe to use and won't burn plant roots. For a quick boost, consider using a leaf fertiliser.

Natural fertilisers

● **Animal manures** provide all the basic plant nutrients, add bulk fibre to the soil and encourage earthworms. Apply them as mulch or dig in to improve the soil.

● **Chicken manure** provides important plant nutrients and makes a good mulch around plants that require lots of fertiliser. Free-range chickens add the manure directly to the garden. Chicken manure is very strong, so age it for at least six weeks before you use it.

● **Seaweed** contains naturally occurring hormones that stimulate root growth. It therefore helps to minimise transplant stress and provides better tolerance to cold and heat. Some kelps are low in nitrogen.

GREEN MANURE

The green manure technique involves sowing specific foliage plants such as winter field beans, buckwheat and lupins, then digging them back into the soil to provide nutrients.

This method has several advantages. While the plants are growing, the soil is protected from major fluctuations in temperature, from drying out and from weeds. As the plants' roots make their way through the soil, they also help to loosen and aerate it.

Once the plants mature but are still soft and green, cut them down to ground level and leave them on the ground for a day or two to wilt, then hoe or dig back into the soil. They will produce humus, which bulks up your soil and supplies extra nutrients.

make it yourself

Liquid manure

Half-fill a bucket with chopped nettles and add rainwater (10 litres of water to 1kg of chopped nettles). Cover the bucket and leave to infuse for 3-4 weeks. Filter the mixture and store in a container. To use the liquid manure, dilute 1 part infusion to 4 parts water. Use the solution to water the roots of plants or to enrich the soil.

Watering

If you adopt wise watering habits and make the most of nature's free water supply you'll conserve a precious resource and ensure that your plants thrive.

Top tips for watering

1 **For very thirsty plants,** sink a large plastic bottle with drainage holes in the bottom in the soil next to the plant and fill with water. It will slowly soak into the soil.

2 **To avoid evaporation,** water only in the early morning or late in the afternoon when it's cool.

3 **It is better to soak the soil** from time to time than to water sparingly every day.

4 **Whenever possible, water the soil not the foliage,** so that the water reaches the roots.

5 **Give plants extra help during periods of drought** and heat. In addition, water more often in windy weather and when plants are actively growing or blooming.

6 **When watering with a hosepipe,** water with a gentle spray. A strong forceful spray can cause stems and branches to break off and flower petals to be damaged.

7 **Collect and store rainwater in water butts.** The downpipes on houses and garden buildings can be modified easily to feed water butts. See page 23.

8 **Use grey water,** recycled from the bathroom and laundry, on your plants provided it is reasonably clean and free from strong detergents. See page 23.

For more tips on saving water in the garden, see page 22.

To reduce loss of moisture through evaporation mulch the surface of the soil when it's moist

Home-grown food

Growing your own food reduces your carbon footprint and can be hugely satisfying. It also allows you to control the number of chemicals in your food.

Vegetables

There's nothing like the taste of vegetables freshly pulled from the earth or picked from the vine. And if grown organically, they're better for you, too.

Vegetable patch know-how

1 **Don't make your first vegetable patch too big.** Start on a small scale, and if you find you need more space, you can extend the area later.

2 **Choose disease-resistant varieties** that will grow well in your climate or conditions.

3 **Sow vegetables successionally** to pack in as much as possible and be able to eat from your plot all year. To give seeds a head start, sow in recycled plastic containers.

4 **Use a mulch between the rows** and between plants to suppress weed growth. If any weeds do appear, pull them up immediately.

5 **Check growing crops daily.** Look out for pests and diseases, and harvest any crops that are ready.

6 **Accept some damage to leaves** and other parts of the plant that you won't eat rather than using chemicals to control pests. Try companion planting (see page 102) as your first line of defence. For extra help, consider using biological controls or introduce some beneficial insects.

7 **Water your vegetable garden in the early morning** or evening, never in the heat of the day as the moisture will be lost through evaporation.

8 **Maximise the use of nutrients** and minimise soil-borne pests and diseases by rotating your crops. Don't grow members of the same vegetable family successively in the same plot (see page 118).

9 **Use flowering plants,** such as lavender, to attract pollinating insects. Planting sweet peas next to runner beans will encourage early pollination of the beans.

MAKING A MINI VEGETABLE GARDEN

● Try the miniature form of carrots, lettuces, peppers, tomatoes and other vegetables that can be grown successfully in containers – even in hanging baskets and window boxes.

● Don't forget that you can garden vertically as well as horizontally! Make a tripod for climbing peas and beans by tying three stakes or bamboo poles together at the top, and then wrapping some wire netting around the stakes.

● If space is tight, grow a salad in a large container. Surround a small-growing tomato with soft-hearted lettuce and clumps of chives.

..... **mature harvest** ....

Spread the harvest by picking some vegetables when they are young and leaving others to mature longer.

10 Buy healthy plants that are sturdy and well-grown, preferably singly in pots, as this will minimise disturbance to the roots when they are planted out.

Selecting the right site

Choosing the best place to grow vegetables is important, as it can make the difference between success and failure.

Shelter Cold winds seriously affect cropping, with even light winds reducing yields by 20 per cent or more. Fences and hedges filter winds and limit their impact, and both can be used to protect vegetables and fruit crops, adding to the total productivity of your garden.

Sun and shade The ideal site for a vegetable patch is an open site that gets sun for most of the day. The majority of crops, particularly winter crops, need plenty of sunlight if they are to yield well. Light shade can be welcome in summer to prevent leafy vegetables such as lettuce, spinach and kohlrabi from drying out, but heavy shade from buildings or trees is best avoided.

Good drainage Heavy, waterlogged soil causes all kinds of problems for vegetables. Before you even think of planting or sowing seeds, dig the site deeply to improve drainage, or consider raising the soil level in beds or ridges to increase the depth of well-drained earth.

Soil Incorporate large amounts of organic material, such as garden compost and rotted manure, which adds body to light soils and opens up heavy clays. In time, with regular cultivating and mulching, your soil and crops will steadily improve in quality.

Size Even a small area can be productive, but your plot size will influence your choice of plants. For a small plot, choose vegetables that can grow close together and include varieties such as beans that use vertical space.

Many traditional heritage and **heirloom varieties** have good disease resistance, crop abundantly **and taste much better**

Crop rotation

An ancient practice, crop rotation is based on the fact that each crop uses different amounts of nutrients and minerals in the soil. Growing vegetables in a new position each year will help to prevent depletion of the soil and the build-up of pests and diseases. Divide the ground into three or four plots or beds, then move groups of vegetables with similar needs and disorders from one bed to the next in annual sequence.

● **The three main vegetable groups** are legumes (peas and beans), brassicas (the cabbage family) and root crops, including onions, with potatoes and squashes in a fourth bed. Wherever there is space, you can fit in salad leaves and sweetcorn.

● **Add rotted manure or garden compost** to each bed when digging and preparing it for planting, depending on the type of crop grown in it (see below).

● **Apply fertiliser** where required (see below), just before planting the crop.

● **In small vegetable plots,** where fewer crops are grown, you can still use rotation. Moving round your crops will improve the health of your plants and help with pest control.

● **Extend a three-year planting cycle** to a four-year cycle by growing green manure on a fourth plot of ground. You can then plant heavy nutrient consumers on this plot the following year.

● **Ideally, carrots, new potatoes, parsley, cucumbers and peas** should only be re-grown on the same spot every six years.

● **As long as they are free of blight,** tomatoes can be cultivated on the same spot for several years provided that you feed them regularly.

● **Keep a record of what vegetables you grow,** sowing and planting dates, treatments given, problems and results for each year. This will provide an invaluable guide for improving your garden's performance next year.

'PIONEER CROPS'

● When you start a new vegetable garden, you may not have time to dig over the whole area and improve all the soil before planting or sowing your first crops but you can use some vegetables as 'pioneers' to help you prepare the soil.

● Jerusalem artichokes and potatoes will break up the soil as effectively as digging.

● Courgettes, pumpkins and cabbages will cover the soil well, suppressing the growth of weeds. They are surface-rooting vegetables so don't need the soil to be well-worked to succeed.

● Avoid sowing onions and carrots as it is more difficult to sow these small seeds into rough ground and they require well-dug soil.

ROTATION GROUPS

	Year 1	Year 2	Year 3	Year 4
Bed 1	Legumes (add well-rotted manure)	Brassicas (add compost and fertiliser)	Roots and onions (add fertiliser)	Potatoes (add manure or compost and fertiliser)
Bed 2	Potatoes (add manure or compost and fertiliser)	Legumes (add well-rotted manure)	Brassicas (add compost and fertiliser)	Roots and onions (add fertiliser)
Bed 3	Roots and onions (add fertiliser)	Potatoes (add manure or compost and fertiliser)	Legumes (add well-rotted manure)	Brassicas (add compost and fertiliser)
Bed 4	Brassicas (add compost and fertiliser)	Roots and onions (add fertiliser)	Potatoes (add manure or compost and fertiliser)	Legumes (add well-rotted manure)

Herbs

Attractive and aromatic, herbs are easy to grow – and growing your own culinary herbs means you won't have to rely on pricey, short-lived supermarket pots.

Choosing the right spot

Most herbs thrive in a warm, sunny position, in well-drained soil and sheltered from cold, drying winds. Some are frost-averse. Grow herbs for cooking fairly close to the kitchen.

● **Plant herbs in the garden,** at random, or as borders.

● **Create a separate herb garden,** planting herbs in rows or a geometric pattern with brick or stone paths.

● **Ensure good drainage:** dig compost or leaf mould into heavy ground, or make a raised bed with well-drained soil.

● **Grow herbs in the vegetable garden.** Rosemary, dill, coriander and lavender will attract beneficial insects.

Tips for healthy herbs

● **Plants under stress from heat or cold will 'bolt'** (go to seed prematurely). To avoid this, select 'bolt-resistant' varieties. Pick off flowerheads as they appear, or the herb will lose its flavour.

● **Grow herbs at the correct time of year.** For example, grow coriander in cooler months, so it develops more slowly.

● **Trim back any damaged growth,** and apply a liquid fertiliser and water to encourage new, undamaged growth.

GROWING HERBS IN POTS

● If space is limited, plant herbs in pots, tubs or window boxes. Use hanging baskets for herbs with a cascading or trailing habit, such as thyme, mint and oregano.

● Another option is a strawberry pot with side pockets. Put low-growing herb varieties, such as thyme, in the pockets and taller ones, such as chives, in the top.

● Invasive herbs (mint and lemon balm) are best grown in containers. A large trough is ideal.

● Annuals such as basil and dill need replacing every year. But even perennials such as mint and sage taste better when young, so renew after three of four years.

HOME-GROWN FOOD

Fruit

You don't have to own a vast orchard to grow your own fruit trees. Many varieties can be planted in a small or modestly sized garden – and some will thrive in pots, if you water and feed them regularly.

Choosing the right site

Local climate is probably the strongest influence on the type of fruit you can grow. Although you can relieve the effects of high rainfall with efficient drainage, and compensate for too little rain by improving the soil and watering, other factors are critical to productivity.

● **In cold gardens,** note where frost lingers longest and plant elsewhere; never plant at the bottom of a slope, where cold air tends to collect. If you have no choice, plant taller fruit trees and late-flowering bush fruit varieties in the cold spots, reserving the warmer sites for smaller and earlier flowering plants.

● **Pick a sheltered site.** Strong winds discourage pollinating insects, injure flowers and cause fruits to drop prematurely. The best protection is a windbreak of netting or open-board fencing, a hedge of beech or a row of trees.

● **Think about the sun and shade.** Warm-climate crops, such as peaches and apricots, and late ripening tree fruit need the most sunshine, whereas most soft fruits will tolerate some shade for up to half of the day. You can train certain fruits on a fence or wall, thereby saving space and allowing the fruits to benefit from the reflected warmth of the sun. Avoid areas of deep shade, especially under overhanging trees.

● **Most soils are suitable for growing fruit,** provided that they are well drained. You should dig heavy clay deeply to prevent waterlogging and work plenty of compost or well-rotted manure into light soils to improve water retention.

Planting a fruit tree

Fruit trees are best bought and planted in late autumn. They will then have the entire winter to put down the new roots they'll need for their growth in spring.

● **Select only those with healthy bark,** a good root system and well-balanced branches in good condition.

● **When buying a stake** to support your young standards, choose one that is about the same thickness as your arm and long enough to sit just below the crown of the tree once it is hammered into the ground. Char the part that will be buried to help prevent it from rotting.

After planting a fruit tree, **rub off flowers** that appear in its first season to encourage **new shoots to grow**

..... **insect hedges**...........
Plant **flowering and fruiting hedges** such as crab apple, bay laurel and elderberry to **attract beneficial insects**

• **Before you plant your tree,** place a large stone in the bottom of the planting hole. It will serve as a wedge that prevents the tree sinking when the hole is filled in and the soil firmed down.

• **Create good drainage in heavy, waterlogged soil** by building up a mound of soil to which you have added well-rotted compost. Then plant the tree in the mound so that its neck is 10–20cm above the surrounding ground level.

• **Protect the bark of newly planted trees from frost** by wrapping the trunks with straw.

Tips for healthy fruit trees

A perfect and inexpensive way to secure a young trunk to a stake or for training or supporting a branch is to use old nylon stockings or tights. They form a wide, soft tie, and will not cause damage to the growing trunk.

• **Remove competition for water and nutrients** by keeping the soil round the bases of young trees free of grass and weeds.

• **The fruits on a tree mature at different rates.** This means picking should be carried out on several occasions, harvesting only the mature fruits from the tree each time.

• **Bees play an essential role in pollination** and have been a feature of the orchard since cultivation began. Beekeeping is a specialist hobby, but if you do want to take it up it will benefit your fruit trees and provide you with delicious honey.

• **Planting colourful flowers and herbs** among the fruit will help to attract beneficial insects, birds and bees.

• **All tits are gardener's friends** because they have voracious appetites for the insect pests that plague fruit trees. Encourage a family of tits to take up residence in your garden by putting up a nesting box among the branches of susceptible trees (see page 104).

• **Pruning once a year** is the best way to ensure that you get the most out of your fruit trees. It opens up the tree to allow the maximum sunlight to reach the fruit.

POTTED FRUITS

Strawberries are perfect for growing in containers but careful watering and feeding are essential to produce a good crop. Apples, apricots, peaches and nectarines can all be bought ready-grafted on to a semi-dwarfing rootstock, making them suitable for growing in pots. Plant fruit trees in a terracotta pot rather than a plastic one for better protection from frost.

THE RIGHT TIME TO PICK

To get the best from your fruit trees, you need to know when to harvest fruits.

APPLES Harvest early varieties as needed, when the first apples begin to fall. Twist the stems of cooking apples; they are ready to pick if the fruit comes off easily.

PEACHES AND APRICOTS These are ready to pick when the fruits soften slightly and yield to the touch.

PEARS If pears are left to ripen completely, they become dry and pulpy. Harvest early varieties when the flesh just yields to the touch. Varieties for cooking or preserves are ready if the fruits come off easily when their stems are twisted.

PLUMS As with pears, plums for cooking and preserves should be picked just before they are fully ripe, when they are still a little firm. Leave eating varieties on the tree until they are fully ripe.

QUINCES Pick quinces in October, when they are yellow and aromatic, and before the cold winter weather arrives. They will finish ripening while they are in storage.

Eco-friendly organisations and suppliers

Use this list of contacts to help you choose products that are not polluting to the environment in their manufacture or use, or that will help you to make your home more energy-efficient.

GENERAL

Department for Environment, Food and Rural Affairs (Defra)
www.defra.gov.uk
Tel: 08459 335577

Forest Stewardship Council
www.fsc-uk.org
Tel: 01686 413916
Information on timber products made from sustainably managed forests.

Friends of the Earth
www.foe.co.uk

Government Environment Agency
www.environment-agency.gov.uk
Tel: 08708 506506

The Green Shop
www.greenshop.co.uk
Tel: 01452 770629
Natural and eco-friendly products from water-saving devices to non-toxic cleaners.

Lakeland
www.lakeland.co.uk
Tel: 015394 88100
Supplies many green products including can crushers, recycling aids, dryer balls and soap nuts.

Natural Collection Catalogue
www.naturalcollection.co.uk
Tel: 0845 3677001
Home furnishings and garden products made from organic materials.

BUILDING MATERIALS AND INSULATION

Association for Environment Conscious Building
www.aecb.net
Tel: 0845 4569773

Centre for Alternative Technology (CAT)
www.cat.org.uk

Natural Building Technologies
www.natural-building.co.uk

Second Nature UK Ltd
www.secondnatureuk.com
Tel: 01768 486285
A supplier of Thermafleece sheep's wool insulation.

The Green Building Store
www.greenbuildingstore.co.uk
Tel: 01484 461705
Energy-efficient products, including spray fittings and flow restrictors for taps and showers, natural paints and water butts.

FENSA
www.fensa.org.uk
Information on the Building Regulations thermal performance standards for windows and doors.

Glass and Glazing Federation
www.ggf.org.uk
Tel: 0870 0424255

Passivent Ltd
www.passivent.com
Tel: 0161 962 7113
Natural and energy-efficient ventilation.

Excel Building Solutions
www.excelfibre.com
Tel: 01685 845200
Building products made from sustainable or recycled materials including Warmcel insulation.

SOLAR POWER

SolarCentury
www.solarcentury.co.uk
Tel: 020 7803 0100

Greenshop Solar Ltd
www.greenshop-solar.co.uk
Tel: 0845 2235440

Solar Twin Ltd
www.solartwin.com
Tel: 0845 1300137

GREEN ENERGY SUPPLIERS

Many energy suppliers offer green tariffs but these offer the most eco-friendly deals.

Ecotricity
www.ecotricity.co.uk
Tel: 08000 326100

Good Energy
www.good-energy.co.uk
Tel: 0845 4561640

Green Electricity Marketplace
www.greenelectricity.org
Information on green energy suppliers and a tarif comparison.

WATER AND ENERGY-SAVING APPLIANCES

Save-a-flush bags
www.save-a-flush.co.uk

Hippo watersavers
www.hippo-the-watersaver.co.uk
Tel: 01989 766667

Rainharvesting Ltd
www.rainharvesting.co.uk
Tel: 0845 223 5430
Suppliers of irrigation systems for gardens, which collect rainwater run-off from roofs and gutters in an underground tank.

Niagara Corporation Ltd
www.niagaracorp.com
Tel: 0870 474 0173
Water conservation appliances.

Eco Kettle
www.ecokettle.com
Tel: 01273 494943

Monodraught Ltd
www.sunpipe.co.uk
Tel: 01494 897700
Information on the sunlight pipe, a system which which pipes natural daylight from the rooftop into your home.

SEDBUK
www.boilers.org.uk
Database of seasonal efficiency of domestic boilers in the UK.

Carbon 300
www.carbon300.co.uk
Tel: 020 7731 8762
Energy-efficient heating & hot water systems.

ENERGY-SAVING ORGANISATIONS

Energy Saving Trust (EST)
www.energysavingtrust.org.uk
Tel: 0800 512012
Information on energy-saving products and grants for home improvements (see right).

Warm Front Hardship Fund
www.warmfrontgrants.co.uk
Tel: 0800 6128735
Details of government grants for energy-saving home improvements (see right).

National Home Energy Rating Scheme
www.nher.co.uk
Tel: 01908 672787
Provides a detailed energy audit of your home.

The National Energy Foundation
www.nef.org.uk

GRANTS FOR IMPROVING YOUR HOME'S EFFICIENCY

The Government, local authorities and many energy providers offer grants to homeowners to encourage them to install loft or cavity wall insulation, or to make other energy-saving improvements to their property. Schemes are all means-tested and how much you can claim depends on your personal financial circumstances.

● The Government's Warm Front scheme (known as Warm Homes in Northern Ireland, Warm Deal in Scotland and the Home Energy Efficiency Scheme in Wales) provides up to £2,700 in England (the maximum varies elsewhere) to householders who install better insulation or draughtproofing, who fit thermostatic radiator valves or who replace their boiler.

● As part of the Government's Energy Efficiency Commitment, all energy providers over a certain size are required to set and achieve targets for improved domestic energy efficiency. Contact your energy provider, who will visit your home and carry out an energy survey, suggest improvements and provide information on grants available.

● All local authorities run schemes to help homeowners towards the cost of making energy-efficient home improvements. Contact your local council by telephone to request information or search their website for details.

● For more information on grants, contact the Energy Saving Trust or Warm Front Hardship Fund (see contact details, left).

DECORATING AND FLOORING

The Alternative Flooring Company Ltd
www.alternativeflooring.com
Tel: 01264 335111
Suppliers of natural flooring, carpets and rugs in jute, coir, sisal, seagrass or wool.

Simply Bamboo
www.simplybamboodirect.co.uk
Tel: 0845 2220408
Suppliers of easy-to-install, eco-friendly bamboo flooring.

EarthBorn paints
www.earthbornpaints.co.uk
Eco-friendly natural paints, varnishes and flooring products.

Auro
www.auro.co.uk
Suppliers of natural decorating products, from paints and wood finishes to furniture polish and floor care products.

Ecos Organics
www.ecospaints.com
Solvent-free paints and varnishes.

CLEANING PRODUCTS

Simple Green
simplegreen.co.uk

Natural Eco-Trading
greenbrands.co.uk

Ecover Cleaning Products
www.ecover.com

BABIES

National Association of Nappy Services
www.changenappy.co.uk
A washing service for dirty nappies.

The Green Baby Company
www.greenbaby.co.uk
Environmentally friendly baby products.

RECYCLING

Rebat
www.rebat.com
Recycling batteries.

Computer Aid International
www.computeraid.org
Supplies unwanted computers to developing countries.

The Cartridge Recycling Scheme
www.cartridge-recycling.org.uk
Recycling printer cartridges.

Recycling Appeal
www.recyclingappeal.com
Recycling printer cartridges and mobile phones.

Oilbank
www.oilbankline.org.uk
Recycling oils.

Recoup
www.recoup.org
Recycling plastics.

Community Repaint
www.communityrepaint.org.uk
Accepts unused paint for community projects.

Community Recycling Network
www.crn.org.uk

NRU
www.nru.org.uk
Links to sites with information on recycling everything from glass to electronic equipment.

RecycleNow
www.recyclenow.com
Locates your nearest recycling point.

Wastewatch
www.wastewatch.org.uk
Information on recyclling and waste treatment schemes.

Ebay
www.ebay.co.uk
The premia online auction site.

Freecycle
uk.freecycle.org
A web-based recycling organisation that allows you to pass on unwanted items or pick up items from others in your area.

SwapXchange
www.swapxchange.org
A site that enables you to swap unwanted items with others around the country.

GARDENING

The garden suppliers below provide everything from compost bins and bird feeders to organic pest controls and water butts.

Greenfingers
www.greenfingers.com
Tel: 0845 345 0728

Green Gardener
www.greengardener.co.uk
Tel: 01603 715096

Organic Catalogue
www.organiccatalog.com/catalog
Tel: 0845 1301304

Wiggly Wrigglers
www.wigglywrigglers.co.uk
Tel: 01981 500391

Henry Doubleday Research Association
www.hydra.org.uk
Advice on growing your own food organically.

RSPB
www.rspb.org.uk
Tel: 0845 120 0501
Definitive information on gardening from the experts.

Index

Acknowledgements

© RD = Reader's Digest Association, all artwork=© Reader's Digest Association
T =Top, B =Bottom, L =Left, R =Right, C =Centre

Front Cover ShutterStock, Inc/Wayne R ● **Spine** ShutterStock, Inc/Wayne R ● **Back Cover TL** Corbis/Elyse lewin/Brand X, **TR** Photolibrary Group/Juliette Wade, **BL** Digital Vision, **BR** ShutterStock, Inc/Baloncici ● **1** ShutterStock, Inc/Wayne R ● **2** www.photodisc.com ● **3** ShutterStock, Inc/Wayne R ● **5 T** iStockphoto.com/Stéphane Bidouze,**TC** www.stockbyte.com, **BC** ShutterStock, Inc/Dan Harmeson, **B** ShutterStock, Inc/Tomasz Pietryszek ● **7** Digital Vision ● **8** ShutterStock, Inc/Baloncici ● **9** © Reader's Digest ● **10** Corbis/Elyse lewin/Brand X ● **12,13** © Reader's Digest ● **15 T** iStockphoto.com/Gordon Ball, **B** ShutterStock, Inc/Nicola Gavin ● **16** ShutterStock, Inc/Sklep Spozywczy ● **17** iStockphoto.com/Alan Chao ● **18** © Reader's Digest ● **19** Alamy Images/Paul Glendell ● **21 T** Corbis/Dex Images, **B** iStockphoto.com/Deniz Unlusu ● **22, 23** © Reader's Digest ● **25** iStockphoto.com/Sherri Camp ● **27** Jupiter Images/Comma Image ● **28** iStockphoto.com/Glen Teitell ● **29** © Reader's Digest/Martin Cameron ● **31** ShutterStock, Inc/Tomasz Trojanowski ● **32** ShutterStock, Inc/Andresr ● **34** ShutterStock, Inc/MaxFX ● **36** Digital Vision ● **37** ShutterStock, Inc/Baloncici ● **38** iStockphoto.com/Kutay Tanir ● **39** ShutterStock, Inc/Stefano Tiraboschi ● **41** ShutterStock, Inc/Thomas & Amelia Takacs ● **42 T** www.styleplantation.com, **C** © Reader's Digest, **B** www.photodisc.com ● **43 L** ShutterStock, Inc/Aridna de Raadt,**R** iStockphoto.com/Edward Shaw ● **44** www.stockbyte.com ● **45** © Reader's Digest ● **47** © Reader's Digest/Ulrich Kopp ● **48 L** © Reader's Digest/Udo Loster, **R** © Reader's Digest ● **49** iStockphoto.com/Janice Richard ● **50 L** ShutterStock, Inc/Ronald Sumners, **R** © Reader's Digest ● **52** © Reader's Digest ● **53** iStockphoto.com ● **55-59** © Reader's Digest ● **60** Digital Vision● **61** Corbis/Reed Kaestner ● **62** iStockphoto.com/ Terence Keller ● **63** iStockphoto.com/Yvan Dubé ● **64** iStockphoto.com/Stéphane Bidouze ● **65** ShutterStock, Inc/Diego Cervo ● **66** © Reader's Digest ● **68** ShutterStock, Inc/Good Mood Photo ● **69** Digital Vision ● **70** © Reader's Digest/Udo Loster ● **72** iStockphoto.com/ _pela Letonja ● **73, 74** © Reader's Digest ● **75** ShutterStock, Inc/Christopher Nagy ● **76** ShutterStock, Inc/Magdalena Kucova ● **77** iStockphoto.com/Yong hian Lim ● **78** iStockphoto.com/ Mary Schowe ● **79** iStockphoto.com/Yong Hian Lim ● **80** iStockphoto.com/Teresita Cortés ● **81** © Reader's Digest ● **82** ShutterStock, Inc/Adam Lu ● **83 T** ShutterStock, Inc/Andi Berger, **B** Brand X Pictures ● **84** PhotoAlto ● **85** iStockphoto.com/Revecca Grabill ● **86** Alamy Images/Jennie Woodcock/ Bubbles Photo Library ● **87 T** iStockphoto.com/ Denise Torres, **B** © Reader's Digest ● **88** Photolibrary Group/Janet Seaton ● **89 T** iStockphoto.com/ Christina Richards, **B** iStockphoto.com/Laura Neal ● **90 L** ShutterStock, Inc/AJT, **R** ShutterStock, Inc/Mashe ● **91** Digital Vision ● **93** ShutterStock, Inc/Sharon D ● **94** Photolibrary Group/Jo Whitworth ● **95** ShutterStock, Inc/Tomasz Pietryszek ● **96** The Garden Collection/Derek Harris ● **97** © Reader's Digest/Sarah Cuttle ● **98** © Reader's Digest ● **99** © Reader's Digest/Debbie Patterson ● **100** ShutterStock, Inc/Tomasz Pietryszek ● **101** Alamy Images/Arco Images Gmbtt ● **102 T** iStockphoto.com/ Robert Smith, **B** © Reader's Digest ● **103** © Reader's Digest/Debbie Patterson ● **105** ShutterStock, Inc/Manfred XY ● **107 T** ShutterStock, Inc/Ariel Bravy, **B** Alamy Images/Blickwinkel ● **108** ShutterStock, Inc/ Daniel Gilbey ● **109** © Reader's Digest/Mark Winwood ● **110** ShutterStock, Inc/C Daveney ● **111 T** © Reader's Digest/Mark Winwood, **B** The Garden Collection/Andrew Lawson ● **112 T** © Reader's Digest/Mark Winwood, **B** iStockphoto.com/amanda Rohde ● **113** © Reader's Digest/Sarah Cuttle ● **114** Photolibrary Group/Michael Davis ● **115** iStockphoto.com/ Schelinski Waldemar ● **116** © Reader's Digest/Debbie Patterson ● **117** The Garden Collection/Nicola Stocken Tomkins ● **119** © Reader's Digest ● **120** ShutterStock, Inc/Sergey Baykov ● **121** The Garden Collection/Liz Eddison

The logos on page 5 are reproduced with the kind permission of the following organisations: The Energy Saving Trust, The Soil Association, Organic Food Federation, Organic Farmers and Growers Ltd, Forestry Stewardship Council UK (© 1996 FSC A.C.), The European Commission.

The Green Home is based on material in *1001 Easy Ways for Earthwise Living*, published by Reader's Digest (Australia) Pty Limited, and *Reader's Digest Energy-Efficient Home Manual*, *Secrets and Tips from Yesterday's Gardeners*, *Hints and Tips from Times Past* and *Garden Basics: Slugs, Pests & Diseases*, all published by The Reader's Digest Association Limited, London.

First Edition Copyright © 2008
The Reader's Digest Association Limited, 11 Westferry Circus, Canary Wharf, London E14 4HE
www.readersdigest.co.uk

Editor Caroline Boucher
Art Editors Louise Turpin, Julie Bennett
Assistant Editor Liz Clasen
Consultants Simon Gilham, Gill Chilton
Proofreader Ron Pankhurst
Indexer Marie Lorimer

READER'S DIGEST GENERAL BOOKS
Editorial Director Julian Browne
Art Director Anne-Marie Bulat
Managing Editor Nina Hathway
Head of Book Development Sarah Bloxham
Picture Resource Manager Sarah Stewart-Richardson
Pre-press Account Manager Dean Russell
Production Controller Sandra Fuller
Product Production Manager Claudette Bramble

Origination Colour Systems Limited, London
Printed in China

ISBN 978 0 276 44379 4
BOOK CODE 400-382 UP0000-1
ORACLE CODE 250012535H.00.24